O R C A

JIM BORROWMAN / NOOMAS
PHOTOGRAPHY

ORCA

VISIONS OF THE KILLER WHALE

Peter Knudtson

FOREWORD BY DAVID SUZUKI

GREYSTONE BOOKS

Douglas & McIntyre Publishing Group
Vancouver / Toronto / Berkeley

Text copyright © 1996 by Peter Knudtson
Photographs copyright © 1996 by photographers credited
First paperback edition 2004

04 05 06 07 08   5   4   3   2   1

Greystone Books
A division of Douglas & McIntyre Ltd.
2323 Quebec Street, Suite 201
Vancouver, British Columbia
Canada V5T 4S7
www.greystonebooks.com

National Library of Canada Cataloguing in Publication Data

Knudtson, Peter.
    Orca

    Includes bibliographical references and index.
    ISBN 1-55054-500-0 (bound)   1-55365-034-4 (pbk.)

    1. Killer whale. I. Title.
QL737.C432K68 1996   599.5'3   C96-910078-7

Library of Congress Catologing-in-Publication data is available.

The following publisher has given permission to use quoted material:
From *The Religion of the Kwakiutl Indians* by Franz Boas. Copyright ©1930
by Columbia University Press. Reprinted with permission of the publisher.

Editing by Nancy Flight
Cover design by Jessica Sullivan
Text design by DesignGeist
Cover photograph by © Amos Nachoum/CORBIS/MAGMA
Printed and bound in Hong Kong by C & C Offset Printing Co. Ltd.
Distributed in the U.S. by Publishers Group West

We gratefully acknowledge the financial support of the Canada Council for the Arts,
the British Columbia Arts Council, and the Government of Canada through the Book
Publishing Industry Development Program (BPIDP) for our publishing activities.

PAGE IV:

JIM BORROWMAN/NOOMAS

PHOTOGRAPHY

PAGES VIII/IX:

FLIP NICKLIN/MINDEN PICTURES

TO THE SMALL COMMUNITY OF INDIVIDUALS

AROUND THE WORLD WHO HAVE QUIETLY DEVOTED THEIR

LIVES TO THE WELL-BEING OF WILD KILLER WHALES

AND TO MY NEPHEW BEN, MY GREAT-NEPHEW, KEVIN, AND MY

NEPHEWS AND NIECES UNBORN

CONTENTS

FOREWORD   *xi*

PREFACE   *xv*

PROLOGUE: INTRODUCING ORCA   *1*

CHAPTER 1   **REMEMBERING ORCA** *9*
Early Descriptions of Killer Whales and Dolphins *10*
A Kwakiutl Vision *13*
A Mythical Haida Sea Monster *15*

CHAPTER 2   **ORCA ORIGINS** *21*
The Evolution of Whales *22*
The Killer Whale Family Tree *23*
Races of Killer Whales *28*

CHAPTER 3   **SHAPED BY THE SEA** *33*
Anatomy of a Blowhole *34*
Breathing and Diving *38*
Heat and Cold *39*
Colours and Contours *43*

CHAPTER 4   **ORCA SOCIETY** *53*
A Matriarchy of Whales *54*
Courtship and Mating *57*
Birth of a Killer Whale Calf *58*
Seasons of a Killer Whale's Life *65*
Cooperative Feeding on Herring in Norway *66*
Hunting Blue Whales in Mexico *69*
Hunting Seals in Argentina *71*
Killer Whale Communication *75*

CHAPTER 5   **IMAGINING ORCA** *83*
The Killer Whale's Brain *84*
Killer Whale Senses *86*
Echolocation: Pictures of Sound *88*

EPILOGUE: HONOURING ORCA   *95*

SELECTED REFERENCES   *104*

INDEX   *109*

A Kwakiutl killer whale mask by
Richard Hunt. COURTESY OF THE
ROYAL BRITISH COLUMBIA MUSEUM,
CATALOG NO. 16460. REPRODUCED
BY PERMISSION OF THE ARTIST.

WE WERE ON A SAILBOAT RETURNING TO PRINCE

RUPERT, BRITISH COLUMBIA, AFTER A WEEKEND

WATCHING GRIZZLY BEARS IN THE KHUTZEYMATEEN

VALLEY WHEN SOMEONE SHOUTED, "WHALES AHEAD!"

I RUSHED TO THE DECK WITH MY THEN TWELVE-YEAR-

OLD DAUGHTER SEVERN. SHE WAS ECSTATIC WHEN WE

SPOTTED THE FINS AND BACKS OF THREE MAGNIFICENT

ORCAS CLOSE TO THE BOAT. THEN THEY DOVE, AND WE

anxiously scanned the water, scarcely breathing as we watched for them to re-emerge. After an interminable wait, I saw them surface far away, near the horizon.

"Look, there they are!" I exclaimed. I looked down at Severn, expecting to find her brimming with excitement. Instead, she was weeping.

"What's wrong?" I asked in surprise.

"Look how far they went in one breath," she wailed, "and we keep them in such a small pool in the aquarium!" With all the innocence of childhood, Severn had hit on the terrible truth about our captive whale program and questioned our entire relationship with the rest of nature.

Staff of aquariums, marine parks and zoos often justify the display of captive wild animals by saying that they play an important role in educating the public. Thus, it is argued, two or three whales are a small price to pay for increased popular appreciation of the animals because it will ultimately lead to an enlightened electorate that will help protect the whales.

Even if we ignore the age-old debate about whether the ends ever justify the means, we must ask what message we receive from watching captive whales. When they perform "tricks" they have learned from their trainers, the animals merely reinforce the message that humankind reigns supreme over the natural world. And what do we learn about the life and behaviour of creatures that are beautifully honed by evolution to roam over vast distances and that share tight familial and social bonds, which we barely understand? The intelligence of orcas is undeniable, so we must wonder what psychological and physiological trauma confinement inflicts on them.

The hollowness of our rationalizations for keeping whales in captivity becomes clear when we perform a simple thought exercise. Suppose a space ship from another galaxy swept up a few human beings to take back home for display. What kind of "information" could be gleaned from looking at the captives held in barren cells? They might be "happy" to perform tricks on cue to relieve the tedium, but it is clear that this confinement would be fundamentally cruel and would only generate artificial behaviour.

Severn's lament highlights the rapid change in public attitudes and perceptions over the last few decades. The need to dominate nature and wild creatures has been replaced by respect, awe and even love. The whale, a highly intelligent animal with a complex communication system and social structure, was an ideal symbol when the United Nations convened the first global conference on the environment in Stockholm in

1972. "Save the Whales" became the rallying cry of a growing environmental movement.

Paul Spong was one of the first people to publicly declare that there was a spiritual dimension to whales and to our relationship with them that demands that they be released from captivity. Today few aquariums would justify capturing more orcas, and many animals now in captivity are no longer made to jump and perform like circus animals. There is widespread awareness of the intelligence of orcas, along with a welcome shift in thinking that balances our infatuation with whales with the discoveries of science.

This magnificent book reveals the long relationship between humanity and whales, assembling our knowledge about them from many different perspectives. Human beings and nature have been on a dangerous collision course in this century. The fate of orcas will tell us whether our species can learn that we must share the earth with other species, not compete with them. After all, as the aboriginal peoples of this land knew so well, orcas are our relatives, worthy of our respect and love.

David Suzuki
Vancouver, British Columbia

Killer Whale by Haida artist Robert Davidson. Like other master artists, Davidson uses both ancient and new elements in this work. REPRODUCED BY PERMISSION OF THE ARTIST

ORCA: VISIONS OF THE KILLER WHALE IS A REFLEC-

TION OF MY OWN PERSONAL SEARCH, BOTH AS A

WRITER AND AS A BIOLOGIST WHO ONCE STUDIED

MARINE MAMMALS, FOR A CLEARER UNDERSTANDING

OF THE ELUSIVE CREATURE WE CALL ORCA, OR THE

KILLER WHALE. THIS BOOK IS BY NO MEANS INTENDED

TO BE AN ENCYCLOPEDIC DESCRIPTION OF THIS SPECIES.

Nor is it meant to "tell" readers how they "ought" to think about an animal that in this era of popular Hollywood films like Free Willy and profitable marine zoos like Sea World has recently so captured the public imagination. Rather, it is simply a collage of fleeting glimpses into the killer whale's world, focussing on a selection of topics that are richly documented in the literature or that have otherwise proved especially illuminating to me.

This kaleidoscopic view of the killer whale is the book's organizing principle. The book begins with a prologue that provides an introductory portrait of the killer whale. Each chapter offers a slightly different perspective on the killer whale's identity. Chapter 1 looks at this creature through the lens of humankind's ancient, prescientific bonds with orcas and their cetacean cousins, with particular emphasis on Native cultures of the Pacific Northwest coast of North America, where killer whale stories and symbols of orcas continue to this day to shimmer with mystery and meaning.

The next three chapters examine the killer whale's world through the lens of modern science. Chapter 2 describes the ancient evolutionary origins of the killer whale. Chapter 3 examines some of its vital anatomical, physiological and behavioural adjustments to an aquatic life. And Chapter 4, in some ways the book's core, explores aspects of the killer whale's extraordinarily complex social organization, as well as this animal's remarkable ecological adaptability as a top marine predator in diverse marine ecosystems around the world.

Finally, Chapter 5 boldly ventures into such challenging topics as the killer whale brain, senses and echolocation apparatus, which demand that we supplement scientific fact with informed leaps of the imagination.

Although I have observed orcas on a number of occasions in both Alaska and British Columbia, I have, by necessity, relied heavily on the pioneering studies of a handful of respected killer whale researchers around the world. I am particularly indebted to the publications of Kenneth Balcomb, the late Michael Bigg, Lance Barrett-Lennard, Graeme Ellis, John Ford, James and Sara Heimlich-Boran, Craig Matkin, P. F. Olesiuk and Paul Spong, among others.

I would also like to express my gratitude to Graeme Ellis and John Ford for generously agreeing to review my text. Any factual errors that may have escaped their keen eyes are of course my responsibility alone.

The heartbeat of this book lies in its beautiful photographs. They represent the labours of these gifted photographers: Kelley Balcomb-Bartok, Jim Borrowman, Chris Cheadle, Adrian Dorst, Jeff Foott, John Ford, Victoria Hurst, Thomas Kitchin, Frans Lanting, Jon Murray and Flip Nicklin. I salute them and their superb images.

Finally, I would like to express my gratitude to my talented editor, Nancy Flight, for the pleasure of working with her again after so many years, and to the book's fine designer, Gabriele Proctor.

INTRODUCING ORCA

THEY SAY THE SEA IS COLD, BUT THE SEA CONTAINS

THE HOTTEST BLOOD OF ALL, AND THE WILDEST,

THE MOST URGENT . . .

THE RIGHT WHALES, THE SPERM-WHALES, THE

HAMMER-HEADS, THE KILLERS.

THERE THEY BLOW, THERE THEY BLOW, HOT WILD

WHITE BREATH OUT OF THE SEA.

—D. H. Lawrence, *Whales Weep Not*, 1947

AT SUNSET ON A JULY EVENING, AGAINST A BACKDROP OF BLUE SKY STREAKED with molten orange and red, I stood alone on the shore of an uninhabited island off the northeastern coast of British Columbia's Vancouver Island, scanning a stunning vista of sea, forest and snow-capped mountains in Blackfish Sound. For the past several days, I had been kayaking solo through this kelp-embroidered rain-forest archipelago in search of northern resident killer whales on their annual summer influx into the area to feed on vast runs of migratory salmon. To my joy, I had spotted the blows of a dozen or more orcas from my kayak as I made my way across the swirling tidal currents of Weynton Passage, en route to Blackfish Sound, which bears one of the orca's local names. And in the rosy light, I now paused to gaze out over the wind-tossed seas, in the hopes of catching one last glimpse of a killer whale before I returned to my tent for the final night of my journey.

Suddenly my heart leaped. There, a few hundred metres offshore and heading directly towards me, were the towering, 2-metre-tall (6-foot-tall) dorsal fins of three adult male orcas, along with the smaller curved one of a female or juvenile male. The four fins protruded out of the water like the stout branches on a drifting log, teetering eerily as the whales swam. I jumped into my kayak and paddled swiftly towards them for a clearer view. Pausing for a moment amid the pounding waves, I sat utterly transfixed by a natural spectacle that would be routine for the fortunate few killer whale researchers around the globe who are privileged to spend hundreds of hours each year in the company of wild killer whales.

Travelling swiftly in tight formation, the quartet of big, sleek black-and-white dolphins surfaced repeatedly to breathe and dive—aquatic dancers in an exquisitely choreographed ballet. At one point, without missing a beat, one of the big bulls raised his shiny, bulging head slightly to glance at me with one eye. Then, apparently undisturbed by my presence, the whales surged on, eventually diving in graceful synchrony to swim out of sight beneath my drifting kayak.

A few moments later, they resurfaced behind me. Pivotting my craft for a final look, I watched the whales proceed swiftly down a narrow channel separating the island on which I was camped from its neighbour and disappear. I could not know what killer whale thoughts they might have been thinking. But it seemed to me that except for the fleeting curiosity one had displayed, they had been all but indifferent to my presence. As the mist from their blows settled, the rhythm of their explosive breaths continued to boldly punctuate the night air.

FACING PAGE:

By lobtailing, or loudly slapping its tail flukes on the surface of the sea, a killer whale produces a resounding whack that is rapidly transmitted under water and may, in some situations, serve as a threat or an alarm signal. JIM BORROWMAN/NOOMAS PHOTOGRAPHY

A human being can never fully grasp the interior reality of another life form. We are biologically fated to perceive the world through the filter of a distinctively human brain and sensory apparatus. For example, although orcas are endowed with keen sight, sound provides most of the information necessary for their survival. As a result, the lives of killer whales, like our own, are one more sensory island in nature's vast archipelago of animal worlds.

In our quest to try to understand animals, few subjects present a greater challenge than does *Orcinus orca*, the killer whale. For within the order Cetacea, the great lineage that includes all living whales, porpoises and dolphins of the world, as well as their aquatic ancestors, the killer whale, or orca, in many ways reigns supreme. In all its swift, stunning black-and-white splendour, it is a social predator par excellence and the inheritor of a spectacular array of evolutionary gifts.

With its enormous brain and well-developed nervous system; with its sophisticated biosonar system for "seeing" its surroundings with sound; with its cavernous, spike-toothed maw, its sleek torpedo shape and its breathtaking size, strength and speed; with its extraordinary intelligence, behavioural adaptability, vocal communication skills and complex social organization—it remains a predatory sea mammal without peer.

Beyond this, there is also the killer whale's sheer physical presence. There is its daunting size: adult males reach 9.5 metres (30 feet) in length and weigh up to 8000 kilograms (17,600 pounds); adult females measure 5.5 to 7 metres (18 to 23 feet) and weigh 2500 to 4000 kilograms (5500 to 8800 pounds). There are its dazzling black-and-white markings: its ebony body and contrasting white belly, along with flashing white blazes behind each eye and a drabber grey "saddle patch" straddling the back. And there is its towering dorsal fin—reaching a height of up to 1.8 metres (6 feet) in mature males. (The dorsal fin is considerably shorter and more crescent shaped in both females and subadults.)

The killer whale also ranks as one of the most widely distributed of all of the more than eighty species of warm-blooded, air-breathing whales, porpoises and dolphins that comprise the cetacean clan. One of the only mammals that has a wider geographic distribution is *Homo sapiens*.

Orcas have been sighted, if not always in large numbers, in virtually every major ocean and sea on the planet. They range from the inky Arctic waters off the shores of Alaska, Greenland and Norway to the tepid tropical seas of the earth's equator and to

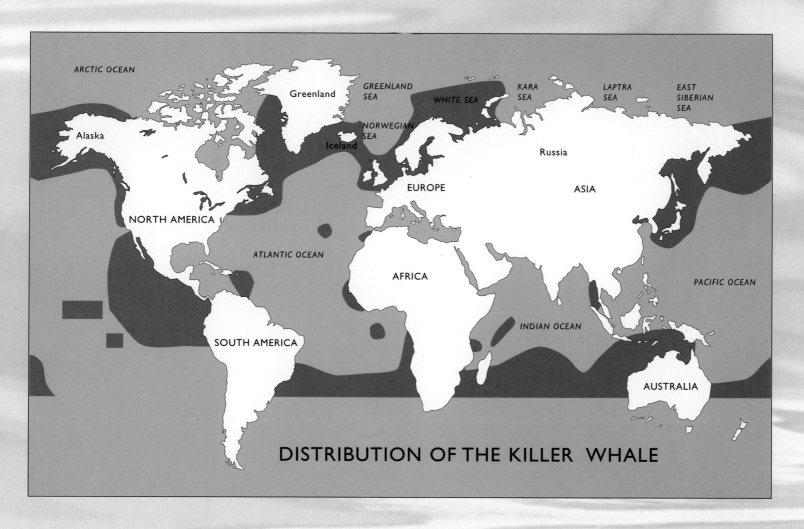

DISTRIBUTION OF THE KILLER WHALE

ARCTIC OCEAN

Greenland

GREENLAND SEA

WHITE SEA

KARA SEA

LAPTRA SEA

EAST SIBERIAN SEA

Alaska

NORWEGIAN SEA

Iceland

Russia

EUROPE

ASIA

NORTH AMERICA

ATLANTIC OCEAN

AFRICA

PACIFIC OCEAN

SOUTH AMERICA

INDIAN OCEAN

AUSTRALIA

ADAPTED FROM C. MATKIN AND

S. LEATHERWOOD 1986, P.44

the frozen fringes of Antarctica. But the greatest concentrations of killer whales by far can be found in the higher temperate latitudes of both hemispheres, particularly in the fertile coastal waters less than 1000 kilometres (600 miles) from shore that lie along the continental margins.

Given such a cosmopolitan range, it is not surprising that killer whales occur in a variety of subtly different physical and behavioural forms. And each regional orca population feeds on its own particular spectrum of marine prey, reflecting local food resources as well as the distinctive dietary preferences of particular groups.

Along the Pacific Northwest coast of North America, for example, a behaviourally distinct race of "transient" killer whales hunts seals, sea lions, porpoises and other large, warm-blooded prey. Yet within their range lives another race, "resident" killer whales, which appear to be reproductively isolated from the mammal-devouring transients and which follow the seasonal bounties of migratory salmon and other local fish.

Off the coast of Norway, killer whale populations are known to thrive on seasonal influxes of herring. Argentine orcas beach themselves in lightning-fast raids on local sea lion rookeries, and there are Arctic orcas known to feed on fish or prey on seals by bumping them off tipsy ice floes. Elsewhere, opportunistic orcas have been reported to devour everything from tropical turtles, dugongs and manatees to oceanic squid and seabirds, and others routinely attack such formidable prey as humpback and gray whales—all to satisfy a daily food requirement estimated at about 4 per cent of their body weight.

Like the wolf and other legendary carnivores, the killer whale has also endured, until quite recently, an exaggerated reputation as the very embodiment of predatory blood lust and teeth-gnashing terror. Simply by christening it "killer" (a whaler's nod to the ruthless efficiency with which some types of orcas assault big baleen whales), we have forever branded this species with a quasi-criminal moniker—one that associates it not just with other big, fierce predatory animals but also with the most despised and debased members of our own species. Even the more neutral term "orca," an increasingly acceptable alternative in many circles, still harbours, in its linguistic links to ancient Roman underworld deities, a hint of the innately diabolical.

The killer whale is an extraordinary creature. But, in many ways, despite recent advances in our knowledge, we still scarcely know it. Our ignorance can be traced in part to the fact that killer whales spend about 95 per cent of their lives under water and therefore largely out of human sight. What little knowledge we have of this complex creature is based on descriptions derived, for the most part, from the tiny iceberg tip of their lives that we are ordinarily privileged to witness.

Seven years after the original publication of this book, the killer whale continues to fascinate us and researchers continue to try to solve its mysteries. Scientists working in the Pacific Northwest, for example, are uncovering tantalizing new clues to the intricacies of orca behaviour and social structure. And they are trying to track the still-uncertain seasonal movements of resident, offshore and transient populations of killer whales in these often-stormy and fog-enshrouded waters.

Some puzzles, such as the recent decline in the southern resident population of orcas—reportedly 17 per cent between 1995 and 1999 alone—are more disturbing. Current scientific consensus suggests multiple causes for this decline, including the decreases in local salmon populations, the accumulation of toxic pollutants (especially PCBs) in killer whale tissues and the delayed reproductive effects of the capturing of female orcas from local populations several decades ago.

There is also the irony that those of us who most cherish orcas may, in our eagerness to see this stunning creature up close, be contributing in a small way to its demise, as boatloads of well-meaning whale watchers routinely disrupt orca communication, echolocation, feeding patterns and movements. Sensible viewing guidelines, if enforced, might lessen such effects, but our sheer numbers threaten the balance. An estimated half million orca watchers depart from the ports of Victoria, British Columbia, and Friday Harbor, Washington, alone, each season, and in peak season dozens of boats and hundreds of tourists might encircle a single pod.

What are we orca aficionados really searching for? I suspect it is something more than the thrill of sighting the silvery plume of a killer whale's prodigious breath or its towering dorsal fin knifing shark-like through the sea. Rather, what we are increasingly drawn to may be the fleeting glimpse of a wild beast possessed of such astonishing grace, intelligence and power that it makes us realize, if only for an instant, that we are mere participants in the natural world, not its masters.

That is why Northwest Coast Native mythology, which often beautifully complements biology by distilling the very essence of these animals, is so important to understanding killer whales. And that is why I wrote *Orca*.

OVERLEAF:
Our knowledge of killer whales comes mostly from the tiny iceberg tip of their lives that we are able to see. JIM BORROWMAN/NOOMAS PHOTOGRAPHY

CHAPTER ONE

REMEMBERING ORCA

THE WOLF IS A BEING OF GREAT ORDER AND . . .

IT KNOWS WHAT MEN DO NOT: THAT THERE IS NO

ORDER IN THE WORLD SAVE THAT WHICH DEATH

HAS PUT THERE.

—Cormac McCarthy, *The Crossing*, 1994

EARLY DESCRIPTIONS OF KILLER WHALES AND DOLPHINS

IN HIS BOOK *OF WOLVES AND MEN*, A CLASSIC STUDY OF THE LONG, UNEASY bond between human beings and wolves, author Barry Lopez recounts a Haida tale about the mythical origin of orcas. The tale tells of a pack of clever wolves that lived along the shores of the Pacific Ocean and learned to go out to sea and prey on big baleen whales. Before long, they were slaying so many whales that the beach was littered with steaming piles of fetid corpses.

On seeing such gluttony, the creator grew furious and unleashed a series of fierce storms to prevent the ravenous wolves from destroying any more whales. As the winds raged, the wolves found themselves trapped at sea and unable to find their way back to the safety of the shore. Condemned to forever feed on oceanic whales in order to survive, they were forced to adapt their ingenious terrestrial hunting strategies to their new aquatic surroundings. In this way, some Haida say, they became the first killer whales: wolves of the sea.

Over the centuries, the killer whale has been held in high regard by a number of ancient, indigenous cultures around the world and, in some cases, has been protected by special hunting taboos. Before the birth of Christ, for example, the Nazca of coastal Peru built temples in honour of kindred killer whale spirits and incorporated killer whale symbols into pottery and other art objects. And local cetaceans, including orcas, were honoured by indigenous peoples as geographically far-flung as the Ainu of Japan and the aborigines of Australia.

Spiritual connections between humans and killer whales flowered most abundantly in Native cultures of the Pacific Northwest coast of North America, where orca populations live in protected coastal waters and are unusually accessible for most of the year. In addition, some traditional Native hunting and fishing strategies in this region offer intriguing parallels with those of their cetacean counterparts. For here, human and killer whale societies have relied for millennia on some of the very same seasonal food resources—protein-rich runs of Pacific salmon, as well as other fish, seals, baleen whales and sea mammals—for their very survival.

In pre-Christian times, Greek and Roman thinkers often lyrically referred to local Mediterranean dolphins as intelligent, compassionate, even divine denizens of the sea. Seen by some as the embodiment of reincarnated human souls, they were looked upon as sacred and worthy of strict protection.

Other observers were more pragmatic. Aristotle properly looked upon dolphins not as fish but as bonafide mammals that, like humans, had lungs (not gills), gave birth to live young and nourished their offspring with milk. In *Historia Animalium*, written in the fourth century B.C., Aristotle also estimated the duration of dolphin pregnancy and marvelled at the impressive social affinity among dolphin family members, particularly between mother and young. Pliny the Elder, writing in the first century A.D., refers to the killer whale directly, describing it as "an enormous mass of flesh armed with savage teeth" and, in reference to its habit of preying on other cetaceans in the area, "an enemy of other whales," willing to "charge and pierce" mothers and calves like "warships ramming."

Early Christian paintings sometimes depicted the biblical scene of Jonah being swallowed not by a great whale but rather by a dolphin. Dolphin symbols surface repeatedly in a variety of mythological settings, adorning images of Netherlands North Sea goddesses, for instance, as well as other European sea deities and guardian spirits. Later, in European heraldry, dolphin icons were sometimes accompanied by the motto *Fistina lete,* meaning "hasten slowly," and medieval Christian folklore often designated the dolphin as a bearer of souls of the dead to a distant oceanic isle of the blessed.

Over the past few centuries, attitudes towards killer whales held by whalers, as well as by naturalists who accompanied them, were coloured by their spectacular sightings of orca attacks on some of the same great whales they were pursuing. As a result, these attitudes sometimes reflect a mix of horror and fascination. An account penned in the early nineteenth century, for instance, portrays the killer whale as possessed of both "deliberate cunning" and a "singular intelligence." And another, written fifteen years later, categorically condemns orcas as "exceedingly voracious and warlike."

In 1874, in his published journals of sailings off the west coast of North America, Captain Charles Scammon declared that the killer whale is, by nature, "intent upon seeking something to destroy and devour." And more than one hundred years later, the writings of famed French oceanographer Jacques Cousteau remind us that this species' fearsome reputation remained fairly intact, even among scientists, until very recently. In his book *The Whale: Mighty Monarch of the Sea*, Cousteau describes a casual encounter with killer whales in the Indian Ocean in 1967—at a time when "we, along with the rest of the world, considered killer whales to be the most fearsome creatures of the sea, the avowed enemies of all life forms to be found in the water, including divers."

Cousteau sheepishly notes that this routine sighting had, in retrospect, left both him and his crew unnecessarily filled with fear.

Historically, the commercial whaling industry itself has never viewed killer whales as prime targets, since they lacked marketable baleen plates and provided little oil. Still, as records show, many thousands of orcas were harvested during this century by Norway, Japan, the former Soviet Union and other countries—intentionally, incidentally to other whale catches or supposedly for "scientific studies"—until the species finally won a measure of protection from the International Whaling Commission in 1982.

Not until the 1960s, when North Americans first began to see performing dolphins on television and live killer whales in public aquariums, was public consciousness about killer whales fundamentally transformed. For the first time, large numbers of people were able to witness for themselves that orcas were not just intelligent, highly social and superbly equipped for life in the sea but also often inexplicably curious about, even affectionate towards, human beings.

This experience, combined with growing public concern about environmental issues, quickly cast the killer whale in a wholly new light. In a sense, we had come full circle: like some ancient, nature-based societies, we had begun to form a relationship with this species based, if not on spiritual kinship, at least on genuine respect.

Today the killer whale can be said to occupy a place in human thought comparable only to that of its terrestrial counterpart, the wolf. Like the wolf, the killer whale has surfaced in the popular imagination as arguably the single most recognizable and revered mammal in its realm.

A KWAKIUTL VISION

IN THE ANCIENT KWAKIUTL COSMOS, ROOTED IN THE FIORD-FISSURED COASTLINE of southwestern British Columbia, killer whales, along with wolves, bears, beavers, eagles and ravens, occupy an especially honoured place. Their status is reflected in the Kwakiutl, or Kwakwaka'wakw, people's use of stylized images of such animals on their traditional animal crests, symbolizing an enduring covenant and a shared ancestry

FACING PAGE:

Tlingit hat. Native traditions have long honoured the killer whale, in part because it is seen as a prodigiously gifted creature, capable, with each breath, of gracefully bridging aquatic and terrestrial worlds.
COURTESY OF THE THOMAS BURKE MEMORIAL WASHINGTON STATE MUSEUM, CATALOG NO. 1–1436.

between humans and these life forms that extend back to the creation. Beyond this sacred kinship with the Kwakiutl people, each of these species is also believed to share a number of vital characteristics with human beings.

For example, like humans, each of these species lives a social existence. Each communicates with others of its kind by using sound. Each has a voracious appetite, and each is a hunter—a predator, relying, at least at times, on a diet of flesh (although, for beavers, "flesh" is a living, soul-laden tree, and for eagles and ravens it includes carrion).

Kwakiutl identification with killer whales is also heightened by the fact that both resident orcas and humans eat salmon, a revered prey species. In fact, because congregating salmon are believed to mirror human society, they are thought to spiritually link all three species, as a fixed reservoir of souls circulates freely between life forms in what the Kwakiutl view as an endless cycle of reincarnation. So by following and feeding on annual migrations of spawning salmon in British Columbian waters, orcas are, in some sense, revealing the humanity that flickers beneath their rubbery black-and-white skin. In fact, Kwakiutl tradition envisions orcas as former human beings who, by donning magical masks and robes, have simply transformed themselves into the whales western scientists refer to as *Orcinus orca*.

The killer whale is also held in high esteem because of its aquatic lifestyle. Like other local warm-blooded, air-breathing sea mammals—sea otters, seals and sea lions, porpoises and dolphins, the immense mysticete, or whalebone, whales—it navigates gracefully between two realms: air and sea. Although orcas seldom intentionally venture very far up a shore, they do retain, in their bodies and habits, memory of their ancient terrestrial ways. They are destined forever to rise rhythmically to the sea surface to breathe air. And they are known to plunge right through the thin, reflective membrane that separates these two neighbouring worlds as they hurtle their huge bodies skyward in an athletic leap, or breach.

To a traditional Kwakiutl eye, the sight of such an airborne sea beast offers irrefutable proof of the orca's true nature. For killer whales, whom the Kwakiutl consider to be the proud chiefs of all dolphins and porpoises, thereby reveal their capacity to freely penetrate the boundary between two worlds—a feat that in any creature is an expression of great power. It is a gift that entitles orcas to participate, the Kwakiutl say, in sacred winter ceremonies just like their own—not only in the killer whale's own undersea home but also up above, on land, in the company of their kin, the Kwakiutl people, who have always deeply admired and revered them.

A MYTHICAL HAIDA SEA MONSTER

THE HAIDA OF NORTHWESTERN BRITISH COLUMBIA HAVE ALWAYS BEEN ASTUTE observers of animals that inhabit both the lands and seas in the vicinity of their ancient island home of Haida Gwaii. So it is not surprising that, along with other neighbouring First Peoples, they long ago recognized important parallels, as well as differences, between killer whales, wolves and themselves.

Orcas, wolves and humans all reign as supreme predators within their respective marine and terrestrial realms. All are highly intelligent, learn and remember with ease and transmit much of their acquired knowledge to their young. All are extraordinarily social creatures, drawing on rich repertoires of behaviour and operating within the boundaries of highly ordered societies. All are respected for their speed, their strength and their sensory powers, and all are steeped in qualities—such as extreme devotion to kin, subtle capacities for social communication and a bent for cooperation.

There is also considerable overlap in the kinds of prey that these three life forms have long relied on in order to survive. Both orcas and humans, for example, eagerly feed on salmon and other ocean-dwelling fish. And wolves and humans alike relish the flesh of freshly killed birds, rabbits and other warm-blooded terrestrial fauna.

Given such common ground in character, appetite and activity, is it possible that all three species have somehow emerged with fundamentally similar, however distinctive, strategies for survival? This idea is encoded in the ancient Haida tradition of oral literature. In their stories, the Haida sometimes speak of a primordial figure known as Wa-'sg,o', a mythic Haida monster, possessing not only the head and body of a wolf but also the fins of a killer whale. And through this hybrid beast, said to dwell in the murky depths of certain local lakes, the Haida seem to be fusing the traits of these two predators that they most admire and identify with.

According to Haida storytellers, when Wa-'sg,o' grows hungry, it satisfies its ferocious hunger by swimming out to sea, through subterranean routes connecting lakes and seas, in search of whales to eat. Upon finding them, Wa-'sg,o' slays them with a spear that protrudes from its nostrils, and then it simply plucks their gargantuan carcasses from the waves with the ease of a fisherman landing a salmon. It places its prey in a neat row on top of its head, right between its wolf ears, sometimes storing up to ten whales at a time in this way. If it is unusually famished, it might carry an additional whale or two in its canine jaws. Finally, propelled by its huge, fan-shaped killer whale flukes, and with its curled canine tail held high, Wa-'sg,o' swims swiftly back home.

Excerpt from a Kwakiutl Prayer to a Dead Killer Whale

"Great Supernatural One. What has made you unlucky . . . Now, you great and good one, have you been overcome by the one who does as he pleases to us, friend. I mean this, that you may wish that I shall inherit your quality of obtaining easily all kinds of game and all kinds of fish, you Great Supernatural One, friend, you Long-life Maker."

Haida Killer Whale by Bill Reid.
REPRODUCED BY PERMISSION OF THE ARTIST

The storytellers say that Haida hunters and fishermen stood in awe of Wa-'sg,o's prowess as a master predator. So on occasion they set out to enhance their own predatory powers by seeking spiritual encounters with the magical beast. On such a vision quest, they say, a Haida hunter first set up camp beside a large lake on Haida Gwaii that was known to be favoured Wa-'sg,o' habitat. Next, he built a special trap to ensnare the monster. He cut down a towering cedar tree, split it lengthwise and bound the two pieces together at each end. Then, with all his strength, he pried the two lengths apart at midpoint and, to maintain the tension, inserted a stout piece of wood between the two lengths. This would serve as the trap's trigger and was baited with a live animal. Then the hunter lowered the huge trap into the water on a line and waited for Wa-'sg,o' to strike. When it did, the hunter quickly reeled in the line and knocked loose the wooden crosspiece, causing the split cedar logs to snap shut on the monster, which would then be dispatched by the hunter.

The hunter's aim was never simply to kill Wa-'sg,o' but rather, through this brave act, to tap into the animal's legendary reservoir of power. After slaying Wa-'sg,o', the hunter promptly skinned the animal. Donning the skin as a robe, the hunter would find his own frail human capacities magically enhanced by Wa-'sg,o's supernatural blend of animal strengths and sensibilities—at once whale-like and wolf-like.

In this way, the hunter, in effect, transformed himself into a new order of being. Importantly, he accomplished this feat by mirroring nature, by reenacting the elemental bond between "eater" and "eaten"—one that permeates and imposes order on the whole natural world. And in so doing, he had now magically alloyed the traits of a human hunter with those of Wa-'sg,o': its awesome size, strength and spirit, and a keen mind, memory and sensory capacity to match.

FACING PAGE:

The average life span of a female orca is estimated to be about fifty years (although many probably live well into their sixties, seventies and even eighties in the wild). For males, the average may be closer to thirty years. JEFF FOOTT/JEFF FOOTT PRODUCTIONS

Traditional killer whale motifs adorn this Tlingit pipe. Today, the killer whale, like the wolf, has surfaced in the popular imagination as arguably the single most recognizable and revered mammal in its realm.
COURTESY OF THE THOMAS BURKE MEMORIAL WASHINGTON STATE MUSEUM, CATALOG NO. 2.5E561

PAGE 20:
Despite their fierce demeanour, killer whales, like wolves, are inclined to treat other members of their extended family fairly gently. When aggressive encounters do occur, they may involve nudging or jaw clapping, or one whale may even rake its teeth across another's back. FLIP NICKLIN/MINDEN PICTURES

CHAPTER TWO

ORCA ORIGINS

MOVING THROUGH A DIM, DARK, COOL, WATERY

WORLD OF ITS OWN, THE WHALE IS TIMELESS AND

ANCIENT; PART OF OUR COMMON HERITAGE AND

YET REMOTE, AWFUL, PROWLING THE OCEAN FLOOR...

UNDER THE GUIDANCE OF POWERS AND SENSES

WE ARE ONLY BEGINNING TO GRASP.

—Victor B. Scheffer, *The Year of the Whale*, 1969

THE EVOLUTION OF WHALES

WE ARE DRAWN TO ORCAS IN PART BECAUSE WE SHARE AN ANCIENT EVOLUTION-ary kinship with them. Like us, orcas are warm-blooded. They breathe air. They possess lungs. They give birth to live young and nurse them with rich, fat-laden milk secreted by mammary glands.

In other words, we are both mammals—members of the class Mammalia. If one traces human and dolphin pedigrees back far enough in time, they do eventually converge. That junction probably occurred some 120 million years ago in the form of a common ancestor, now extinct, that bore scant resemblance to either modern humans or modern dolphins.

This primitive land mammal was a small, furry, rather inconspicuous, shrewlike mammal—an "insectivore," feeding on tiny insects, worms and larvae, as well as vege-tation. From such inauspicious beginnings, over time and in diverse settings, emerged the full array of modern mammals—dogs and cats; hippos, horses and human beings; whales, porpoises and dolphins; and all the rest that we see around us today. Thus, every living mammal—whether it is hoofed or clawed, terrestrial, aerial or aquatic—represents one more brilliant evolutionary variation on a basic mammalian body plan that found its earliest expression in this modest ancestral insectivore.

Life on Earth, in the form of primitive precursors of modern cells, had its first stir-rings in the primeval seas. Slowly, over eons, these ancient protocells evolved into more complex, multicellular plants and animals. Many species remained aquatic; others grad-ually adapted to a more terrestrial existence in what might be called early life's first invasion of land. Killer whales, like all cetaceans, arose from primitive mammals that were already thriving on land. Thus, the remarkable success of whales, dolphins and porpoises as aquatic, air-breathing mammals is the product of a re-invasion of the seas that occurred long after the ancient four-legged ancestors of whales—equipped with hair, lungs, legs, teats and other mammalian traits—had already been striding across the earth for tens of millions of years.

In fact, the terrestrial ancestors of whales were probably relatives of the ancestors of modern ungulates—deer, cattle, pigs and other so-called cloven-hoofed mammals. But whereas the ungulate lineage remained on land, the budding whale lineage invad-ed the virtually untapped ecological opportunities of the sea. It did so tentatively at first, hugging the shallows of equatorial shores, only later becoming gradually committed to a totally aquatic existence.

Reflecting this evolutionary history, modern orcas continue to anatomically mirror those distant times. Although we think of killer whales as sleek and hairless, for example, they, like other cetaceans, do possess hair—the hallmark of the class Mammalia—if fleetingly, during fetal stages of development. Similarly, the orca fetus, like its kin, also transiently displays such other mammalian traits as four stubby limbs, a pelvis and a tail.

In addition, the huge skeletons of orca adults, so hydrodynamically sculpted for aquatic life, are, like our own, simply variations on a fundamental mammalian design. An X-ray image of a killer whale's fore flipper, for instance, reveals a pattern of interconnected arm, hand and finger bones that clearly mirrors ours, even if it is deceptively encapsulated within a rigid paddle of orca flesh, blubber and skin. And although adult orcas have no visible hind limbs, buried deep in the massive musculature of their hindquarters is a set of tiny pelvic bones, evolutionary relics—no longer attached to the spine or even functional—of a time when their ancestors practised more amphibious ways.

Even a killer whale's blowhole, so different, at first glance, from our own nostrils, is nothing more than an evolutionary job of re-plumbing. Over millions of years and countless generations, this opening to the respiratory passages has gradually been relocated from the front of the skull to its present position near the crown of the head.

In short, our sense of kinship with killer whales is rooted in biological fact. Natural selection has reshaped orcas in countless ways to thrive beneath the waves. Nonetheless, they remain, beneath it all, kindred mammals, cloaked in masterful aquatic disguise.

THE KILLER WHALE FAMILY TREE

EVOLUTIONARY BIOLOGISTS SUGGEST THAT THE FIRST TRUE WHALES TO PLY the earth's seas may have made their first appearance on the scene during the Eocene epoch some 53 million years ago. Judging by a fragmentary fossil record, they were relatively small— probably less than 3 metres (10 feet) long—and bore a passing resemblance to killer whales or other modern cetaceans. For example, like land mammals, they drew their breath through primitive nostrils near the tips of their snouts, and some of them still retained the use of their hind legs.

Out of this archaeocete, or ancient whale, stock, perhaps 30 to 40 million years ago, possibly later, emerged the two principal modern branches of the cetacean family tree that today encompass every living species of whale, dolphin and porpoise in the world. One, the odontocetes, or toothed whales, has a diverse membership that includes dolphins and porpoises, and ranges from killer whales, pilot whales, belugas and bottlenose dolphins to narwhals and even the great sperm whale. The other, the mysticetes, or baleen whales, includes all toothless baleen, or filter-feeding, whales, ranging from fin, gray and sei whales to minke and blue whales.

Teeth are absolutely fundamental to the lives of toothed whales. The odontocetes' rows of typically spiky, grasping dentition aid these whales in capturing live marine prey. In contrast, the mysticetes' comb-like baleen sieves passively filter clouds of marine plankton from vast quantities of sea water. Other features also distinguish killer whales and their toothed cousins from baleen whales. Toothed whales have subtly asymmetrical skulls (usually lopsided towards the left), they have a single blowhole, or nostril, rather than two, and they possess biological sonar, or echolocation, a remarkably sophisticated sensory apparatus, comparable to that found in bats. By emitting streams of high-pitched sounds from their foreheads and interpreting the patterns of returning echoes, they are able to scan their surroundings acoustically (in addition to visually, with their eyes) and thus to navigate dim undersea realms with ease, even in total darkness.

Ever since the Oligocene epoch, beginning about 35 million years ago, both toothed and baleen whales have thrived in the ancient seas. But not until about 11 million years ago did the first true dolphins—members of the family delphinidae, to which the killer whale belongs—arise from their ancient toothed-whale ancestors. And, with the development of echolocation, which enabled them to detect and track prey, along with other evolutionary innovations that permitted them to exploit vast, untapped food resources in the sea, these primitive dolphins soon exploded into a stunning diversity of forms.

FACING PAGE:

Rows of conical, interlocking teeth allow the whale to grip slippery marine prey ranging from small fish to great whales in its attempt to satisfy a daily food requirement estimated at 4 per cent of its body weight. FLIP NICKLIN/ MINDEN PICTURES

Groups of resident killer whales often coalesce to form large, seasonal congregations. Resident orcas live in remarkably stable family groups, which are altered only by births or deaths and which are the building blocks of larger pods. JIM BORROWMAN/NOOMAS PHOTOGRAPHY

27

In human affairs, a
"dynasty" is a powerful
family that maintains con-
trol of the rich resources
of a territory through a
continuous successsion of
rulers of the same lineage.
Despite its political conno-
tations, the term may offer
a useful analogy for the
remarkably stable extended-
family groups that make up
resident killer whale society
in the Pacific Northwest of
North America.

Biologists suggest that
social birds and mammals
are most likely to form
large, stable family units—
the very hallmark of resi-
dent killer whale society—
when they control excep-
tionally rich food resources.
That is, offspring are more
likely to remain with one or
both parents beyond sexual
maturity if parents guaran-
tee access to vital resources.
And the striking size and
stability of resident killer
whale pods may arise, in
part, from powerful pres-
sures on adolescent orcas
to linger for a lifetime in

With time, each new species of dolphin became exquisitely adapted to its own local environmental conditions and dietary needs. In the process, this burgeoning cetacean clan eventually gave rise not only to modern killer whales but also to a host of other dolphins—including pilot whales, bottlenose dolphins, and Risso's and white-sided dolphins, to name a few.

In this rich diversity of dolphin strategies for survival in oceans around the world lies the astonishing evolutionary success of the modern killer whale, *Orcinus orca*, and its closest cetacean kin.

RACES OF KILLER WHALES

IN THE JARGON OF EVOLUTIONARY BIOLOGY, A RACE CAN BE DEFINED AS A geographically isolated subpopulation of a species made up of animals that routinely interbreed with one another. In mammalian species, each such race typically not only displays distinctive differences in appearance or behaviour but also lays claim to its own separate region, seldom crossing paths with members of a related form.

Killer whales do not always conform to this pattern. Although orca races living in the coastal waters off the northwest coast of North America, for example, are presumed to belong to a single species—*Orcinus orca*—they apparently do not routinely interbreed. To date, researchers have identified (if not yet fully described) three distinct races of killer whales in this region. And preliminary studies in Alaska, Norway, Argentina, Antarctica and elsewhere around the world suggest that orcas in these areas may exhibit similar, if subtly different, variations from these basic killer whale races, or subspecies.

The first race, known as "resident" killer whales, is by far the best known of the three. Resident orcas have been the principal subject of classic Pacific Northwest killer whale studies, involving the individual identification (based on slight differences in dorsal fins and other body features) of approximately three hundred whales that frequent the inshore waters surrounding Vancouver Island and Puget Sound in the summer months.

These resident killer whales share biological and behavioural traits that distinguish them from their two neighbouring forms. They are highly social and live in extraordinarily stable family social units, which regularly coalesce into larger groups, or pods, composed of up to several dozen kindred animals. They feed exclusively on fish—predominantly on salmon and occasionally on bottom fish. They are very vocal and possess a variety of distinctive repertoires of social calls. While travelling, they tend to dive for brief periods of three or four minutes or less and to navigate directly along ocean passages rather than hugging the shore. Their dorsal fins tend to be recurved, or "windswept," with a fairly blunt tip, and they often display saddle patches on their backs that are slightly marbled rather than uniform white or grey.

In contrast, "transient" killer whales, a second race known to inhabit the same waters, seem markedly less social—usually travelling alone or in much smaller, more loosely structured groups of six animals or less that lack the fixed membership of resident family units. They feed not on fish but predominantly on seals, sea lions, porpoises and other sea mammals. They also spend considerably more time under water than resident orcas—blowing less often and usually diving for five minutes or more. They also tend to be relatively mute, vocalizing rarely as they silently patrol shorelines, stalking their wary prey, and share a single common dialect with only minor regional variations. Finally, their dorsal fins are more triangular and somewhat more pointed at the tip than those of the resident killer whales, and their saddle patches are a more uniform grey rather than marbled.

The precise size and boundaries of regional transient killer whale populations have not yet been determined. But there is mounting evidence that these whales tend to travel widely in small, mobile groups along the entire western coast of North America. Nor has anyone yet deciphered their social structure. But one thing is clear: the range of transient killer whales overlaps with that of local resident killer whales—even though members of these two forms apparently do not interbreed or, for that matter, even socially intermingle.

The third race, only recently identified, is the "offshore" killer whales. They live in large groups, often numbering from thirty to sixty or more animals, and seem to prefer (as their name suggests) open waters to the more protected inshore ones favoured by residents and, to a lesser extent, by transients. Offshore orcas have been sighted, for instance, over the continental shelf near British Columbia's Queen Charlotte Islands and

the company of knowledgeable mothers who provide them with access to abundant local fish stocks and breeding opportunities.

In this sense, one might say that local "dynasties" of resident killer whales emerge over time as generations of mothers and their young, sustained by dense, reliable food resources such as salmon, tend to stay together rather than disperse. In contrast, the more fragile families of transient killer whales—characterized by orca young that are impelled to abandon their natal families to search for more scattered warm-blooded prey such as seals, sea lions and porpoises—simply dissolve each generation.

well off the west coast of Vancouver Island—where they presumably feed largely on fish, including salmon (but possibly also on local marine mammals). In addition, their crescent-shaped dorsal fins with rounded tips and occasionally mottled saddle patches, while resembling those of their inshore resident cousins, remain distinct.

What are we to make of this emerging, but still hazy, picture of genetically distinct yet geographically overlapping races of killer whales in the Pacific Northwest?

Because different races do not, by definition, ordinarily interbreed in nature, it is likely that following a long shared evolutionary past, these three populations of *Orcinus orca* diverged relatively recently, geologically speaking (perhaps a mere 100,000 or so years ago in the case of residents and transients) into separate, reproductively isolated gene pools. Over tens of thousands of years, each of these distinct buds on the killer whale branch of the dolphin family tree has thrived independently despite often overlapping ranges. And in adapting to local environmental conditions and food resources, each has developed its own particular social organization and predatory habits.

As I write, researchers are busy collecting and analyzing DNA from tiny tissue samples harvested from living members of each form in the hopes of finding new pieces to the complex puzzle of orca population dynamics. But until researchers are able to assemble a more complete inventory of biological and behavioural differences, distinctive breeding and dietary strategies, oceanic home ranges and travel routes and—crucially—genetic fingerprints of all three orca races, scientists can only speculate on their possible ancient origins and contemporary interrelationships.

Clues are tantalizingly close. We are on the verge of bearing witness, for the first time, to a documented evolutionary history of killer whales in this region, etched in the ancient genetic messages of orca DNA.

FACING PAGE:

Every orca population is a reflection of a complex interplay of regional evolutionary and ecological forces, including its local history, environmental conditions and available food resources. JIM BORROWMAN/NOOMAS PHOTOGRAPHY

OVERLEAF:

A lone orca bull's explosive exhalation of breath creates a towering plume of pale mist. JIM BORROWMAN/NOOMAS PHOTOGRAPHY

CHAPTER THREE

SHAPED BY THE SEA

ORCINUS ORCA IS AN INCREDIBLY POWERFUL AND

CAPABLE CREATURE, EXQUISITELY SELF-CONTROLLED

AND AWARE OF THE WORLD AROUND IT, A BEING

POSSESSED OF A ZEST FOR LIFE AND A HEALTHY SENSE

OF HUMOR, AND MOREOVER, A REMARKABLE FONDNESS

FOR AND INTEREST IN HUMANS.

—Paul Spong, *Mind in the Waters*, 1974

ANATOMY OF A BLOWHOLE

ONCE UPON A TIME, SCIENTISTS SAY, WHALES HAD NO BLOWHOLES.

For millions of years after ancestors of the first cetaceans had invaded the sea, primitive whales breathed through nostrils located, as in most mammals, near the tip of their snouts. But in a monumental evolutionary change that now characterizes this group, the nostrils gradually began to move from the snout to the top of the whale's head.

This critical transformation did not, of course, take place overnight. Rather, it occurred incrementally, over many thousands of generations. Nor did it take place in splendid isolation; it was only one anatomical change among many, as these air-breathing mammals adapted an unwieldy terrestrial body to the rigours of life in the open sea.

What benefits might a blowhole confer?

First, the migration of the nostrils, along with their underlying plumbing, to the crown of the head, allowed ancestral whales to breathe with greater ease. For the first time, they could rapidly replenish vital respiratory gases, even while they were partially submerged or travelling at high speeds.

Second, coupled with the development of specialized shunts in the respiratory passages that by-passed the oral cavity completely, the relocation of the blowhole also permitted whales to utterly divorce the acts of breathing and eating. Unlike humans, whose respiratory and digestive systems converge in a common tube in the throat, whales can thus effortlessly devour their meals "on the swim"—without ever bothering to hold their breath.

In addition, an expanded network of nasal pouches and passages beneath the blowhole would eventually give rise to the vital social cries and biosonar clicks of many modern cetaceans. And the whales' and dolphins' increasingly efficient mechanisms for holding their breath and recirculating air during deep dives gave their descendants the opportunity to become increasingly verbose—their chatter no longer interrupted by repeated dashes to the surface for more air.

"This, in turn," in the words of renowned American whale expert Kenneth Norris, writing in his book *Dolphin Days*, "freed the dolphin ancestor to live its life as a truly aquatic animal, to dive, explore, feed and evolve its societies with reference to water, not air."

FACING PAGE:

Over millions of years, whales' nostrils have gradually migrated from the tip of the snout to the top of the head to form a blowhole. This change has freed orcas to gracefully swim, dive and feed in their aquatic surroundings while remaining permanently tethered to the terrestrial world overhead.

JIM BORROWMAN / NOOMAS PHOTOGRAPHY

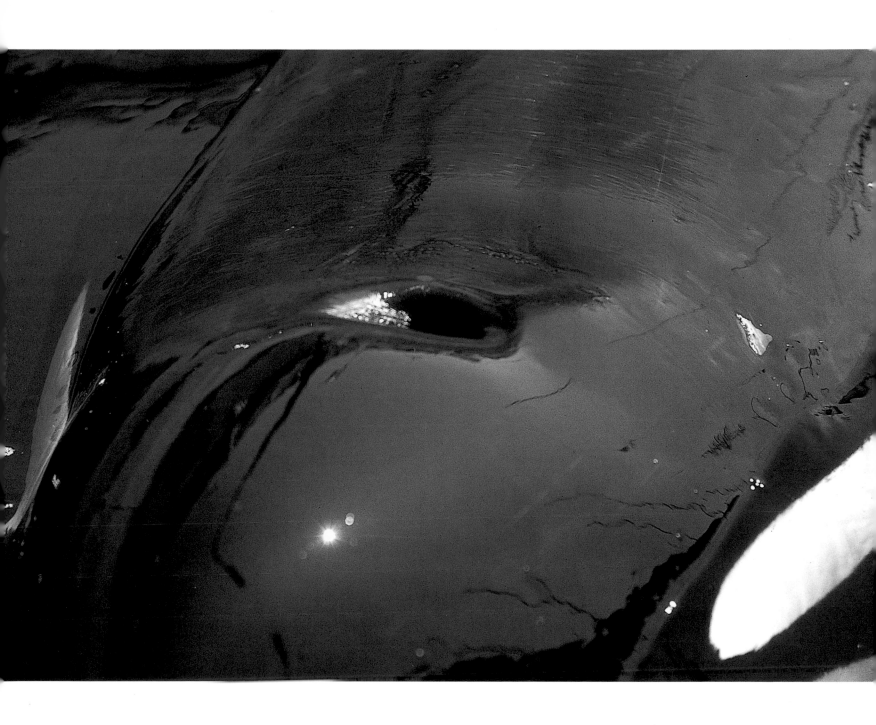

A speeding orca begins to exhale an
instant before its head breaks the
surface of the sea. KELLEY BALCOMB-
BARTOK

Social bonds between orcas are maintained, in part, by distinctive underwater calls that travel more than four times faster than in air and can be heard over distances exceeding 16 kilometres (10 miles). JEFF FOOTT/JEFF FOOTT PRODUCTIONS

*As it swims, a killer whale
displays the athletic grace
of a dancer filmed in slow
motion. Viewed under
water and up close, its
broad, horizontal tail
flukes rhythmically rise
and fall, fanning the dim,
algae-fogged waters. The
whale's huge head, seem-
ingly expressionless, except
for a pair of dark, alert
eyes, rocks up and down
with each powerful thrust
of its flukes.*

*Its long, undulating
spine, buried beneath a
thick blanket of blubber
and muscle, is astonishingly
supple. With each beat of
its muscled hindquarters,
its back arches like a taut
bow and then recoils. Its
big, paddle-like fore flippers, appearing as rigid as
shields, hang motionless
but tilt slightly with each
change of course, steering
the animal like paired
rudders.*

BREATHING AND DIVING

AS AN AIR-BREATHING MAMMAL, A KILLER WHALE WILL DROWN IF IT CANNOT surface periodically to replenish its stores of oxygen. At the same time, its body has been exquisitely shaped by life beneath the sea to dive for as long as several minutes and up to hundreds of metres in depth.

How have orcas managed to reconcile their terrestrial breathing apparatus with an aquatic way of life in which perhaps 95 per cent of their lives is spent submerged?

For one thing, a killer whale, like other cetaceans, manages to get far more metabolic mileage out of each lungful of air than do most terrestrial mammals. It can exchange gases more completely with each breath. It can dive with lungs filled to the limit and then collapse its flexible rib cage as water pressure mounts, squeezing surplus air into the winding nasal passages beneath its blowhole. And it is able to store substantial reserves of oxygen not just in its circulating red blood cells but also in its body fluids and muscle tissues.

During a deep dive, the body of a killer whale also draws on other ingenious biological tricks to stretch its limited stores of oxygen. Its thunderous heartbeat slows down. Its massive musculature keeps on contracting, even at very low oxygen levels. Its circulatory system automatically diverts oxygenated blood to high-priority organs such as the brain, heart and swimming muscles, temporarily depriving others in order to prolong time under water. And if the whale must make a sudden rapid ascent back to the surface, it is able to effortlessly reabsorb excess blood nitrogen, thereby avoiding agonizing bouts of the "bends" that imperil human divers.

Since breathing is usually carried out collectively, it is an act of social solidarity as well as a physiological act. Most terrestrial mammals, including humans, breathe individually rather than in close social synchrony with their fellows. (There are, of course, exceptions. Consider the interlinked inhalations of a quartet of jazz musicians, rhythmically breathing as one as they jam.)

The social dimension of synchronized breathing in killer whales is perhaps most apparent in mothers and their calves. From the instant of birth, an orca mother enters a long and intimate respiratory relationship with her newborn calf, as the calf's first, rapid, bobbing attempts to gulp air gradually become aligned with her breathing. The blows of resident killer whale mothers and calves will continue to be tightly linked throughout their long lives. It is as if (in resident orca society at least) a mother's lifetime of rhythmic breaths has been transformed into a metronome for her mobile family.

Such communal respiration is often discernible as well in larger gatherings of orcas, including entire pods, as they travel, forage or rest. At such times, several matrilineal family groups may coordinate their breathing with others within the pod so that the blows of one whale occur within a few seconds of the blows of another.

In resident orca society, the degree of respiratory synchrony between individuals (and groups) seems to be correlated with the degree of biological kinship between them. If so, the rhythm of breathing could serve as a dramatic behavioural display of family unity, of social familiarity and even of affection among whales.

In this, it is perhaps not unlike our strolls with a loved one, arm in arm, locked not in respiratory synchrony but in synchronized locomotion according to the slow, shuffling gait of a bipedal primate.

HEAT AND COLD

THE COSMOPOLITAN KILLER WHALE THRIVES NOT JUST IN THE COOL TEMPERate waters of the Pacific Northwest or in the more tepid tropical waters but even in the frigid, ice-embroidered oceans of northern and southern polar regions. Its ability to survive in such cold water lies in an array of impressive thermoregulatory, or heat-conserving, adaptations to low temperatures that orcas, like other sea mammals, have evolved over millions of years.

First, there is the killer whale's large body, which, according to the basic laws of geometry, has a smaller proportion of heat-dissipating skin surface per unit of volume than a smaller body. Thus, the killer whale's large size helps it conserve heat.

Second, the basal metabolic rate of a killer whale tends to be set somewhat higher than that of a comparably sized land mammal and so generates a modest surplus of heat.

Third, the body of an orca, like those of other cetaceans, is sheathed in an insulating capsule of blubber, which, like a scuba diver's wet suit, reduces heat loss to surrounding water. At the same time it provides padding to the animal's streamlined form and serves as a vital, high-calorie food reserve for lean months of the year.

The tail flukes themselves are as sleekly crafted as the metallic wings of a light airplane. As the whale turns, they rotate slightly along the axis of the slender, stem-like stalk of the tail called the caudal peduncle—a slim conduit of tendon and bone cables that links "engine" to "propeller."

The flukes are, at times, capable of astonishing dexterity, twisting and flaring to offer additional braking, balance and control. Ordinarily, they pump up and down at a fairly leisurely pace, with long, sustained glides between each beat. But they are capable of rapid acceleration, generating impressive bursts of speed that can exceed 30 kilometres per hour (18 miles per hour).

As they travel, kindred killer whales typically form a breathing group, surfacing, blowing and diving in near synchrony. Such a shared respiratory rhythm is considered by some to be a useful indicator of close social affiliation.

Against the stunning backdrop of
Alaska's pristine Prince William
Sound (before the disastrous *Exxon
Valdez* oil spill of 1989) a solitary
killer whale, for motives unknown,
indulges in a succession of exuberant
leaps lasting for hours. PETER
KNUDTSON

Finally, the killer whale circulatory system automatically minimizes heat loss as the animal cruises through chill waters. For instance, arteries ferrying warm blood from the heart to the dorsal fin, flippers and tail flukes are neatly wrapped in "counter-current" coils of cooler veins, designed to retain some of the heat of hot arterial blood before it reaches the skin surface and is lost forever to the sea. Conveniently, this clever physiological mechanism can also work in reverse. For example, an orca that is patrolling warm tropical waters or that is temporarily overheated can rely on this same mechanism to help cool itself down. Under these circumstances, the venous blood discharges some of the heat picked up from the sun- or sea-warmed skin surface or tired muscles to the cooler arteries.

Although a bull orca's big dorsal fin is, like an elk's antlers, primarily a secondary sex character, it presumably also contributes to the whale's cooling system. The fin is, in either sex, a living radiator designed to dissipate surplus body heat into surrounding sea water or salt air as the great dolphin swims gracefully by.

COLOURS AND CONTOURS

WHY HAS NATURE DRESSED THE KILLER WHALE IN SUCH A CLOWNISH COSTUME of black and white—the black dominating the whale's upper, or dorsal, surface and the white covering portions of its lower, or ventral, surface, as well as dramatically accenting the face with a pair of bright ovoid eye blazes and the back with a drab saddle patch?

We cannot say for sure, but since orcas are apparently not routinely preyed upon by any nonhuman predator, it is unlikely that nature has selected their hallmark monochrome colour scheme because it conceals them from creatures intent on devouring them. As top predators in the marine food chain, however, orcas might be expected to reap considerable evolutionary advantage from any skin coloration that made them more successful in the chase.

Intriguingly, it is possible that the stark black-and-white pattern makes the whale's massive form less recognizable as it moves in for the kill. (Although in an adult

A wild orca "performs" a spectacular
breach. The whale's distinctive, elongated,
hourglass-shaped white genital patch, with
a single black central spot overlying a
retractable penis, identifies it as a male.

male orca equipped with so extravagant a dorsal fin, stealth clearly is already drastically compromised in certain situations.) How might this camouflage work?

First, a killer whale's "invisibility" to prey may be enhanced by the simple combination of dark-coloured back side and light-coloured belly, a form of camouflage common in many marine species, known as counter-shading. The principle is rather simple. A uniformly hued object under sunlit skies appears lighter in colour dorsally, darker ventrally. By reversing that pattern and neutralizing the natural effects of shading, counter-shading camouflage helps an animal shed shadows and fade into its surroundings. Moreover, because the animal's lower surface is light coloured, it tends to blend in with the bright sea surface when viewed from below. At the same time, its dark upper surface tends to merge with the dim ocean depths when viewed from above.

Second, the whale's predatory disguise may, paradoxically, be enhanced by the very aspects of its coloration that strike us as so visually bold. For example, several of the killer whale's most distinctive patches of white skin—its white eye blazes, its white flank markings, its grey saddle patches—appear to be strategically placed to break up and contradict the predictable contours of an approaching predator. By briefly shattering a prey animal's perception of a whale's form, an orca's pinto colour patterns could easily disorient the prey, leaving it vulnerable to attack. That is, if a killer whale's body were a uniform black instead of mottled, a wary salmon might more readily detect its advancing torpedo shape as a threat. But faced with an actual orca, it is, for an instant, tricked into seeing not a dangerous dolphin but a shifting collage of dark masses—until, that is, one of them transforms into a gaping set of killer whale jaws.

It is also possible that a killer whale's colours play an important role in orca social behaviour. Skin pigmentation may, for example, help maintain the orderly, military-like formation of a travelling orca group. For even in dimly lit or murky waters, each animal's brilliant white eye and flank patches may signal its location, speed and orientation, in much the same way that a car's headlights and taillights announce its presence to other drivers on a dark night.

It is even conceivable that orca colour patterns facilitate far more subtle social interactions, just as they do in many social birds and mammals. A white eye blaze may serve, in a sense, as a built-in bull's eye, directing another whale's playful poke or aggressive charge towards a patch of skin safely beyond an easily damaged eye. Similarly, a grey saddle patch might announce a "socially acceptable" body area for

bumping, teeth raking and other rough-house behaviour, without submitting dorsal fins, flukes and other vital appendages to undue risk.

Among killer whales, the sexes are also, to some extent, colour coded. On their lower abdomens, for example, male orcas display an elongate, almost hourglass-shaped patch of white, with a bold, black central spot marking the slit leading to the underlying penis (which retracts neatly inside the whale's streamlined body like a plane's collapsible landing gear). Females, in contrast, have a white genital patch that is stubbier and more oval, emblazoned with a horizontal row of three smaller black spots, highlighting a central vaginal opening, surrounded by a pair of mammary slits (leading to similarly retractable nipples). Field biologists sometimes confirm the sex of killer whales by glimpsing these distinctive geometric markings framing the genital openings. So it does not seem entirely unreasonable that keen-eyed orcas themselves might occasionally do the same.

In addition, these and other sex-linked visual cues may play a part in synchronizing the activities of killer whales during courtship and mating. For example, white areas of the abdomen, along with the undersides of the flukes (broad and slightly curled in mature males) may function as beacons along an airport landing field to help guide an amorous orca bull into a proper belly-to-belly alignment before copulation.

To date, such voyeuristic musings remain speculative. For despite abundant observations of prolonged, sensual, courtship-like interactions between resident orcas, no one has yet published detailed, irrefutable descriptions of actual killer whale matings in the wild.

FACING PAGE:

As a top predator in marine food chains, the killer whale is capable of preying on virtually any creature it chooses. It, in turn, is prey to no other species save *Homo sapiens*.
VICTORIA HURST / FIRST LIGHT

OVERLEAF:

When travelling, an extended family of killer whales typically swims at speeds ranging from a few to more than 10 knots. Their coordinated breathing generally follows a pattern of a relatively deep dives lasting several minutes followed by a series of shallower, more rapid dives. JIM BORROWMAN / NOOMAS PHOTOGRAPHY

CHAPTER FOUR

ORCA SOCIETY

MANY PEOPLE SEEM TO WISH TO BELIEVE THAT WHALES

ARE COMMUNICATING WITH US AT THE DEEPEST

LEVELS. BUT SINCE THE DAWN OF HUMAN HISTORY WE

HAVE ALWAYS GREETED WHALES NOT BY COMMUNICAT-

ING WITH THEM BUT BY KILLING THEM.

A MATRIARCHY OF WHALES

CLASSIC STUDIES OVER THE PAST TWO DECADES OR SO IN BRITISH COLUMBIA and Washington, monitoring hundreds of individually recognizable orcas based on their distinctive body markings, have confirmed that resident killer whales there live in a social organization known as a matriarchy. That is, matrilineal descent—the vertical, intergenerational bonds between mothers and daughters and granddaughters within an extended family—forms the spine of resident killer whale society.

The basic building block of resident killer whale society is the matrilineal, or family, group, made up of a mother, her sons and daughters, and her daughters' offspring. It usually consists of less than ten (but sometimes as few as three or four) individuals. But it commonly embraces three generations, providing continuity and order in resident killer whale society. As American killer whale expert Kenneth Balcomb wryly notes in *Pacific Discovery* magazine, "Dispersal of individuals simply does not occur while mother is alive, and mother lives for a very long time."

This enduring mother-young relationship is the glue that binds up to three or four generations of kindred whales into a mobile, ecologically efficient extended family of predators, with a membership list that is established at birth, is stable over time and lasts for a lifetime. And it is the lifelong bond between an orca mother and the descendants who swim and breathe by her side, acquiring vital skills under her wise tutelage, that transforms killer whale pods into social "circles of learning" for generations of young whales, thereby fostering the whales' survival.

In a healthy population, orca family units flourish, adding new members with each season's fresh bounty of new orca calves. The swollen matrilineal family unit may gradually become unwieldy. Eventually it may fracture along natural matrilineal fault lines when a mother dies or a daughter, increasingly burdened by the demands of her own growing offspring of both sexes, gradually breaks away from her natal group, founding a new mobile matriarchal unit of her own within the pod.

A resident killer whale pod can be defined as a large gathering of kindred family groups that share a complex social, biological and vocal legacy, which biologists have only recently begun to decipher. When a pod periodically dissolves into smaller groups to travel or forage, a given matrilineal family group tends to associate preferentially with certain other families from that pod. A cluster of such affiliated matrilineal family groups is known as a subpod. The members of a subpod all rely on the same basic

Resident killer whale society is
remarkably stable. A mother and
calf form an intimate and lifelong
bond that is the fundamental unit
of orca social organization. KELLEY
BALCOMB-BARTOK

repetoire, or dialect, of social calls, and they travel together throughout their lives.

As veteran Canadian orca researcher Graeme Ellis and co-author Bruce Obee state in their recent book *Guardians of the Whales:* "Subpods, clusters of maternal groups, are 'the constant' in orca society, remaining together for their entire lives. In more than two decades of observation, an orca has never been known to permanently defect from one subpod to another."

This observation is corroborated by killer whale expert John Ford, writing in *Natural History* magazine. "What is especially striking about pod organization is that individuals, and thus their repertoires of calls, seem to stay in the group for their entire lives," he says. "No whale has yet been seen to transfer permanently from one group to another. The pod's large bulls—once thought to be the breeding 'harem masters' of the group—are simply the mature male offspring of the females in the pod."

COURTSHIP AND MATING

ORCAS, LIKE MANY DOLPHINS, APPEAR TO BE EXTRAORDINARILY SENSUAL ANImals. And courtship-like interactions between animals occur not only between possible breeding pairs but also across generations between whales of the same sex—a reflection, perhaps, of the possible role of such social intimacy in somehow neutralizing aggression in these fierce predators.

In the Pacific Northwest, mating among resident killer whales is thought to take place in late summer and fall, when pods in a community seasonally coalesce to form large, animated throngs of up to a hundred or more whales known as superpods. At such times, orcas may engage in an assortment of courtship-like behaviour, including exuberant bouts of chasing and splashing, gentle nudging and stroking, visible erections by males—all punctuated by loud, percussive flipper and fluke slapping. Matings presumably take place quickly between partners from different pods. Thus, fathers are unlikely to travel with offspring and paternity is difficult to trace.

In contrast to killer whale matings, killer whale births have, on occasion, been witnessed in natural settings. Only in artificial settings, however, has the sequence of events in an orca calf's submarine birth been recorded in enough detail to inform the brief birth scenario that follows.

FACING PAGE:

Swimming and breathing by its mother's side, an orca calf acquires crucial survival skills. JEFF FOOTT / JEFF FOOTT PRODUCTIONS

BIRTH OF A KILLER WHALE CALF

THE KILLER WHALE MOTHER, HER LOWER ABDOMEN ONCE SLEEK BUT NOW swollen with the big fetus, is, after sixteen or seventeen months of pregnancy, on the verge of giving birth to a new calf. She restlessly swims about, periodically rising to breathe. Then she pauses for a moment, suspended horizontal and motionless beneath the shimmering surface. Her head and tail flukes lift slightly, bowing her back into an inverted arch and exposing the white patch of her genital area. Her body stretches and then quivers—a huge black-and-white marionette manipulated by unseen hands.

Suddenly, the calf's black-and-white head begins to protrude from her lower abdomen. Although a newborn orca calf is commonly born tail first, this calf is emerging head first. Its blunt snout angles down and back toward her flukes. Although her vagina has already dilated enormously, the calf's passage down the birth canal is blocked at the level of its white eye patches. With each maternal contraction, its head surges out a few centimetres, only to suck back in with each subsequent relaxation.

In an instant, the tension is shattered. The mother accelerates forward and then begins to swim in a wild frenzy. Soaring and spinning, she executes an agonized series of underwater barrel rolls, rotating along the long axis of her body, as if trying to catapult her unborn offspring out of her womb by sheer centrifugal force. At times, she breaks from her manoeuvres to race upside down along the bottom of the pool, flashing her white underbelly towards the surface.

Then her frantic activities reach a climax. In the midst of her acrobatic labour, the calf is jettisoned from her body like a blunt, black-and-white, 2.5-metre-long (9-foot-long), 200-kilogram (440-pound) torpedo. As she swims horizontally, the calf is launched in the opposite direction, red plumes of blood billowing from the freshly torn stem of its umbilicus. No sooner has it broken free than it is swimming fluidly, if clumsily, to the surface to take its first urgent breath of air. As it swims—a slender, miniaturized black-and-white replica of its mother—the calf's triangular dorsal fin droops limply, rippling in the cool turbulence like a banner. Its fore flippers are held rigidly, and its tail flukes, freshly unfurled, flail awkwardly against the water.

As the exhausted mother begins to swim at her usual leisurely pace, the calf dives to rejoin her. It swims at her side, just behind the protective shield of her right flipper. Moving along her abdomen, it soon finds her retractable abdominal nipples and begins to suckle for the first time.

FACING PAGE:

Orca calves are usually born tail first, as shown in this rare photograph.

JON MURRAY / *THE PROVINCE*

ABOVE:

A killer whale's skin has the rubbery
texture of a hard-boiled egg and is
exquisitely sensitive to touch in
some areas. Touch, along with hearing and sight, presumably plays an
important role in maintaining the
intimate, lifelong bond between an
orca mother and her calf. KELLEY
BALCOMB-BARTOK

FACING PAGE:

Like the wolf, the killer whale has,
until quite recently, been burdened
by an exaggerated reputation as the
very embodiment of teeth-gnashing
terror. Traditional Native visions of
orcas often also embrace other,
more redeeming qualities such as its
keen intelligence, clever cooperative
hunting strategies and strong family
loyalties. JEFF FOOTT / JEFF FOOTT
PRODUCTIONS

FACING PAGE:

Classic studies of individually identifiable killer whales in British Columbia and Washington have established that resident orca society here takes the form of a matriarchy. KELLEY BALCOMB-BARTOK

ABOVE:

An orca mother and calf frolic. As intelligent, gregarious mammals, young orca calves routinely play with their mothers, as well as with other extended-family members of both sexes and all ages. JEFF FOOTT/ JEFF FOOTT PRODUCTIONS

SEASONS OF A KILLER WHALE'S LIFE

ORCAS, LIKE HUMAN BEINGS, PASS THROUGH A SUCCESSION OF FAIRLY PRE-dictable biological stages of growth and development as they progress from infancy to mature adulthood. Because resident killer whales are thought to often reach the age of fifty—on occasion sixty, seventy or even eighty—the seasons of an orca's life may offer illuminating parallels to our own.

Infancy among orcas is marked by a number of visible features. Among them: the young calf's characteristic rapid, bobbing, respiratory pattern, the butterscotch tinge to its pale eyespots and belly, its tendency to shed patches of skin during its rapid growth, and its extremely close proximity to its mother, including bouts of riding almost effort-lessly on her slipstream, near her dorsal fin, as she swims.

Although the orca calf is extremely precocious at birth compared with its physi-cally helpless human counterpart, both form an intimate bond with their mothers that lasts for years and during which much of their initial orientation to the world takes place through learning. In resident killer whales, lactation lasts approximately one year; calves begin to learn how to catch fish for themselves as early as six months following birth.

What might be termed orca adolescence also bears certain parallels to our species' own dynamic juvenile and teen-age years. Orca males are generally biologically pre-pared to mate by the time they are twelve or thirteen years old—neatly paralleling puberty in boys. Orca females are likely to reach sexual maturity slightly sooner, just like girls.

During adolescence, members of both species exhibit an exhilarating sense of curiosity about their surroundings. They enter an expanded social world, spending an increasing amount of their time away from parental eyes. And they revel in their newly discovered physical prowess—often expressing their joy in spectacular displays of ath-leticism, social play and sexual explorations. At the same time, youthful killer whales are presumably also acquiring a measure of mastery over vocalizations, echolocation techniques, social protocol and strategies of the hunt.

Even adulthood offers intriguing parallels between the lives of *Orcinus orca* and *Homo sapiens*. For one thing, an orca female has typically given birth to her first calf by the time she reaches fourteen or fifteen, mirroring the onset of motherhood for many young women around the world, in the absence of medical intervention. For another,

FACING PAGE:

Biologists have become adept at iden-tifying individual killer whales in the wild based on distinctive features of each animal's dorsal fin and saddle patch markings. CHRIS CHEADLE/ FIRST LIGHT

according to some studies, orca mothers are fertile (if not necessarily reproductively active) well into their fourth decade and ordinarily give birth to between four and six calves during their approximately twenty-five years of reproductive life. Again, these figures correspond with those for many mothers in human society.

Finally, old age also bears more than a passing resemblance in these two exceptionally social species. In both, these golden years begin when the last of what is usually a succession of offspring has been reared—usually sometime during the fifth or sixth decade of life. Wild killer whales often enjoy surprisingly long life spans. The life span of a typical female orca is estimated to be about fifty years (although some grandmothers probably live well into their sixties, seventies and even eighties); male orcas, like their human counterparts, tend to die considerably sooner than females.

During the twilight of their lives, orcas, particularly matriarchs, provide valuable services to their extended families. An elderly killer whale might, for example, look after young, vulnerable members of the group while a mother is feeding or resting. It might use its prodigious memory to help guide kin quickly and safely to a traditional resting place or seasonal salmon run. It has mastered vital vocal dialects, echolocation skills and hunting strategies and is capable of patiently demonstrating them to the young, who are gifted mimics, in didactic slow motion, if necessary.

COOPERATIVE FEEDING ON HERRING IN NORWAY
THE DIETARY HABITS OF KILLER WHALES ARE AS DIVERSE AS THEIR GEOGRAPHIC surroundings. Orcas are often aptly referred to as "wolves of the sea," in reference not only to their keen minds, social bent and role as top predator but also to their exceptional capacity to adapt to a wide range of environmental conditions and food resources.

Killer whales around the world are known to devour an astonishing array of marine species, ranging from dozens of varieties of fish and assorted seals, sea lions and sea birds to massive great whales. At the same time, orcas can also be specialists. They are masters at honing individual and communal hunting strategies and food preferences in order to exploit huge seasonal pulses of animal prey in a particular region—salmon

FACING PAGE:

Three killer whales, flanked by rooster tails of white spray, engage in a bout of synchronized "speed swimming." Killer whales are capable of reaching speeds of about 30 kilometres per hour (18 miles per hour) as they surge partially, or even completely, out of the water to take a breath of air. JEFF FOOTT/JEFF FOOTT PRODUCTIONS

*As they congregate in prime
feeding areas off the coasts
of British Columbia and
Washington during spectacular summer and fall runs
of migrating salmon,
resident killer whales often
rely on cooperative foraging
strategies. Pod members
fan out across a coastal
passage, travelling abreast
in a loose flank formation
that may encompass several
square kilometres as it
advances up the strait.
The foraging orcas scan
the waters ahead of them
visually and acoustically.
When they encounter
salmon, clusters of whales
may noisily leap or splash,
alerting other members
of the pod to a local abun-
dance of prey. Others may
break ranks temporarily to
pursue their fleet quarry.*

runs in Pacific Northwest waters, for example, young elephant seal in rookeries in the Indian Ocean or gray whale calves along the Pacific coast of North America.

Off the coast of Norway, killer whale populations are known to thrive on seasonal influxes of herring. During the dark months of the Norwegian winter, along the Lofoten and Vesterålen island archipelago, hundreds of orcas congregate seasonally to pursue vast shoals of overwintering herring. Here, in the chill, clear fiords of Norway's north-west coast, with the aid of a remote-controlled underwater camera, researchers have recently made detailed submarine observations of a cooperative killer whale feeding strategy they call "carousel feeding," which is similar to a strategy employed by bottle-nose dolphins in the Black Sea.

It is an exquisite, communal, predatory ballet, acted out almost entirely under water. It begins when a number of orcas join forces and begin to swim rapidly under and around a deep, slightly dispersed school of herring, like a squadron of fighter planes on patrol. Instinctively, the herring panic, crowding closer together until they form a single, densely packed ball—often several metres in diameter—made up of hundreds of fish, each about 35 centimetres (14 inches) long.

Then the squadron of orcas tightens the perimeter of its three-dimensional patrol, at the same time gradually chasing the school towards the surface. Exploiting the herring's natural defensive response, the whales race in increasingly smaller circles around the mobile mass of fish, compacting it further. Vocalizing throughout, the predators dive and soar with astonishing grace, their white eye patches and flank markings flashing like mirrors, accentuating their aggressive movements and further disorienting their prey.

In an aquatic blur, the killer whales and their quarry slowly spiral upwards. Eventually, as they near the surface, some of the orcas begin to porpoise, surging part way out of the water at high speed, white rooster tails of spray in their wake, and then plunging back in. Others slap their great tail flukes against the surface with slow, thunderous whacks. Still others suddenly break formation to dive deep beneath the shifting cloud of herring, swerve and then rocket skyward—displaying their white bellies and under-flukes, like bullfighters' capes, with each pass.

Periodically, a few orcas exhale great luminescent curtains of air bubbles from their blowholes as they circle the herring, sending visible ripples of fear through the group. Others cruise upside down under the fish, preventing easy escape to deep waters. With each whale's approach, the vast cloud of herring contracts and then quickly regains its shape. It twists and swirls, the glittering scales of the fleeing fish flickering in startled synchrony, like the feathers of a flock of shorebirds in flight.

As this gracefully choreographed performance reaches its crescendo, actual feeding begins. Individual whales take turns veering away from their circling patrol to swim directly into the densely packed herring. Often the charge is accompanied by an explosive retort, as the whale delivers a quick, powerful blow to the herring with its tail flukes—leaving a trail of stunned, and often shattered, fish in its wake.

The killer whale then pauses to devour the dead or immobilized herring one by one, while other orcas in the group continue to form a living corral around the remaining fish. After the feeding whale resumes its place, another breaks away from the group to take its turn—attacking, striking and then eating its share of the spoil.

From above, the only evidence of this coordinated frenzy, beyond the occasional rise of black dorsal fins and shiny backs, punctuated by loud blows, are glimpses of the herring in flight. As the orcas feed, they repeatedly stampede the fish to the surface. In their panic, some of the uppermost fish in the school leap completely out of the water, making the waters roil. And each time a whale delivers another whack with its tail flukes (with an explosive impact that, some researchers suggest, may be at once physical and acoustic), the surface waters sparkle with an upwelling of silvery, sequin-like fish scales.

The orca troupe eats its fill and then departs—leaving the surviving herring to retreat to deeper waters. Overhead, a flurry of ravenous sea gulls, kittiwakes and eagles feed noisily on the floating detritus of the fresh kill.

The mobile phalanx is held together, in part, by intermittent vocal exchanges, drawing on the pod's repertoire of a dozen or so discrete calls, supplemented by occasional loud percussive tail slaps, breaches or other long-distance signals. Such dialogue probably provides coherence to the group as it moves from one favoured feeding spot to the next and also helps it to gracefully coordinate turns at aquatic intersections.

HUNTING BLUE WHALES IN MEXICO

AT TIMES, A COORDINATED ATTACK BY A GROUP OF PREDATORY KILLER WHALES on a large warm-blooded sea mammal such as a baleen whale bears an almost uncanny resemblance to a pack of wolves in pursuit of a large terrestrial mammal such as a caribou or moose.

On a warm afternoon, in the sunlit waters not far from the southerly tip of Baja

California, Mexico, a group of killer whales was observed in the midst of a feverish assault on a young blue whale. Approximately thirty orcas chased the solitary 18-metre-long (60-foot-long) baleen whale, swimming parallel to it, at close range, on both sides as it fled. They swam at high speed, lifting white roostertails of water in their wake.

The strategy of the hunt was carried out with impressive precision. Some positioned their powerful bodies (each measuring less than half the length of their massive prey) close beside and parallel to the rapidly swimming and diving whale. Others placed themselves directly ahead of it; still others, directly behind it.

It was as if the orcas had deliberately set out to herd the blue whale, like trained dogs working together to herd a reluctant sheep. Through this coordinated tactic, they were able to control the pace and direction of the whale's flight, disturb the rhythm of its blows and dives, and, by enclosing it in a mobile corral of surging killer whales—their teeth gnashing—terrify it.

By early evening, the ferocious attack was still under way and had carried predators and prey across some 32 kilometres (20 miles) of sea. As the blue whale gradually tired, the killer whales would take turns veering towards the huge animal, tearing long ribbons of flesh from its glistening sides and back with their spiked teeth. Despite these gaping wounds, exposing ragged patches of blood-stained white blubber and painting the roiling waters red, the great rorqual swam on.

But again and again another orca would charge at the exhausted blue whale—peeling off another ribbon of dark skin, ripping another mouthful of bleeding flesh, further weakening the big whale. Finally, more than five hours after the attack had begun, the marauding orcas, for unknown reasons, abandoned their pursuit. Perhaps exhausted, satiated or simply indulging in a tactical respite, the killer whales slowed their pace, dropped their tightly coercive formation and quietly swam away—leaving their severely damaged prey to swim slowly, gingerly, for the moment at least, on its solitary way.

As the blue whale blew and then painfully arched its ravaged back for a shallow dive, a ragged expanse of excavated white blubber lay where its distinctive black dorsal fin had once stood.

HUNTING SEALS IN ARGENTINA

AT PUNTA NORTE, ALONG THE EASTERN COAST OF ARGENTINA, KILLER WHALES do not seem to follow the classic predatory pattern displayed by resident and transient orcas along the Pacific Northwest coast of North America. They do not restrict their diet exclusively to either cool-blooded marine fish or warm-blooded sea mammals but exploit seasonal pulses of both kinds of prey as they become locally abundant.

But if the killer whales of Punta Norte have proved themselves adept at both fishing and hunting, it is their hunting—and specifically, their astonishing ability to stalk, attack and seize vulnerable young seal and sea lion pups right off beaches—for which they (along with orca populations in the storm-tossed Crozet Islands of the South Indian Ocean and elsewhere) are most famous.

The table is set for these opportunistic Argentine orcas when populations of sea mammals return each year to the Punta Norte area to form seasonal breeding rookeries along its shores. Southern elephant seals breed here in October, and a few months later

A killer whale patrols the water adjacent to a steep Argentine beach, stalking plump, young sea lion pups splashing in the shallows. JOHN FORD / URSUS PHOTOGRAPHY

The killer whale is one of nature's
supreme predators and the inheritor
of a spectacular array of evolutionary
gifts. JEFF FOOTT / JEFF FOOTT
PRODUCTIONS

they are joined by hundreds of southern sea lions. Before long, hordes of young, naive pups of both species are making their way into the sea for the first time in their lives. As a result, each year, between about October and March, Punta Norte offers up an extraordinary bounty of tender young seal and sea lion pups to killer whale pods familiar with the ecological patterns of this place.

But the orcas face formidable problems. First, they must hunt at times, tides and coastal sites that offer the best prospects for success. Second, they have to be able to distinguish young seals from their larger, stronger and more experienced adult kin, who not only are less likely to be taken but are also potentially dangerous. And, third, and perhaps most daunting, they must have an attack strategy that enables them to sink their teeth into the plump pups frolicking at the water's edge without becoming fatally stranded themselves.

A core group of about ten orcas, supplemented at times by others, returns to Punta Norte each year, demonstrating that they have mastered all three obstacles to this rich, seasonal food resource. Biologists have recently shown that killer whales do, in fact, efficiently concentrate their assaults at precisely those points along the shoreline where young pups, the preferred prey, are most plentiful. They tend to selectively attack the youngest and most vulnerable animals from any mixed-aged groups of seals or sea lions on the beach. And they have devised a spectacular form of attack that has become, in effect, a local killer whale "tradition."

It is a learned skill that requires a whale, in defiance of all that it has known, to hurl itself, in a potentially life-threatening act, onto dry land. Each orca hunter must polish this skill to perfection—with the help of an older, more experienced family mentor, capable of rescuing it if it should find itself helplessly stranded on land. And each must find ways to pass on its hard-won mastery, sometimes demonstrating the skill in slow motion to young descendants, who are natural mimics.

One killer whale in a pod will often assume primary responsibility for hunting. It patiently patrols the waters parallel to steep pebble beaches in the rookery that are particularly suited to a sudden sneak attack. This orca may be accompanied by a second family member—one perhaps less skilled in the hunt—who, by distracting seals with its tall dorsal fin as it flamboyantly cruises by, will function primarily as a decoy. Relying largely on ordinary hearing, the hunting whale targets a young pup—often distinguishing it from others by the distinctive sounds of its playful swimming and splashing.

Then, in a lightning burst of speed, its dark dorsal fin knifing above the waves, the killer whale suddenly veers shoreward. As it reaches the shallows, it thrusts its massive black-and-white body almost entirely out of water—its tall dorsal fin wobbling, its whole rubbery body throbbing with the effort, as it lurches still higher up the shore.

If the sneak attack has been successful, the whale deftly seizes its unsuspecting prey in its jaws and shakes it vigorously, like a dog with a rag doll. Then, with an agility born of disciplined practice in the company of more experienced whales, it bows its back, pivots around and, with the next wave, slides back into the sea, gripping the hapless pup in its teeth. Meanwhile, behind it, hordes of fellow pups scurry in terror to the safety of higher positions along the shoreline.

Although a successful hunter may take several pups in a day, it does not simply devour them. Rather, it returns to its family group to share its kill. Often a crippled young seal or sea lion will be deliberately turned over to younger orcas in the pod. And as they eagerly torment their prey—indulging in mock pursuit of the still living pup, releasing it, then chasing it, biting and bumping it, sometimes even catapulting it high in the air with a powerful slap of their tail flukes—they are, in nature's eyes, committing no crime.

KILLER WHALE COMMUNICATION

A Dolphin's "Smile"
THE DELIGHTFULLY UPTURNED MOUTH OF THE KILLER WHALE'S COUSIN THE bottlenose dolphin has sometimes been lyrically referred to as a cetacean "smile." Of course, the "smile" is a permanent feature, not a fleeting facial expression.

The heads and faces of killer whales are so contoured and cushioned for a streamlined underwater existence that they are virtually expressionless. Yet killer whales actually possess an impressive repertoire of visual signs and signals with which they can convey to one another a variety of emotional states.

Dolphins convey hostility to one another using a number of often interrelated

FACING PAGE:

An orca conducts a lightning-fast raid on a local sea lion rookery off the coast of Argentina, grasping a fat, unsuspecting pup in its huge jaws in a hunting manoeuvre it has honed to perfection. JEFF FOOTT / JEFF FOOTT PRODUCTIONS

actions. First, the animal might simply face another animal head on. Second, it may conspicuously open its mouth, exposing its sharp teeth, or sometimes noisily clap its jaws together. Third, by arching its back, it may assume a sinusoidal, S-shaped posture—a delphinid threat display that presumably serves to exaggerate its body size.

A dolphin's eyes can also communicate considerable information, just as our own eyes do. For example, veteran dolphin trainers have claimed that captive orcas sometimes express aggression through a reddening of the scleras, or "whites," of their eyes, and that a variety of other very subtle indications of their internal states—from illness to impending mischief—may also be read in their eyes.

Moreover, a dominant dolphin (unlike a dominant primate) typically glances briefly at a subordinate and then quickly looks away. And a submissive dolphin (unlike its primate counterpart) is more likely to stare. As a result, some researchers argue, romantic human observers may occasionally be inclined to naively interpret the steady gaze of a captive killer whale through a glass window as a moving display of interspecies affection, when it might better be described as a cetacean act of contrition.

Orca's Voice

THE ASTONISHING VARIETY OF SOUNDS THAT ORCAS MAKE—FROM SIREN squeals, whistles and other cries to streams of buzz-like echolocation clicks—are produced not in a larynx, or voice box, but in labyrinthine nasal passages located under the blowhole. When the whale inhales, a portion of the air is released back up into the nasal passage linking blowhole and lungs by means of a control valve. This reserve quota of air is forced through the nasal passages, generating a rich range of possible vibrations as it passes over specialized structures; in much the same way, air released slowly from a balloon produces high-pitched squeals.

A killer whale's underwater calls are not normally punctuated by trails of exhaled bubbles, for a diving orca uses recycled air to vocalize. It accomplishes this feat by repeatedly passing its lungful of gases through the network of nasal pipes and pouches—even while it is fully submerged, swimming and thus no longer actively breathing.

It makes sense for killer whales to vocalize in this way. If they had to inhale anew after each brief volley of calls or clicks, they would sacrifice much of their legendary aquatic freedom. Each time they conducted a noisy echolocation survey of their surroundings or indulged in an excited family chorus of shrill cries following a submarine feast of salmon, they would find themselves suddenly breathless. Forced to break off these activities and quickly ascend for a fresh gulp of air, one of the sea's most exuberantly social mammals would discover that its world was tethered even more tightly to the membrane separating ocean and atmosphere.

Orca Accents

ORCAS COMMUNICATE WITH EACH OTHER USING A VARIETY OF DISTINCTIVE calls that resemble high-pitched squawks, whistles or squeals. Members of an orca population share a proportion of the recognizable "discrete calls," or at least fragments of them, within this general "vocabulary" of sounds. But pioneering studies carried out by Canadian acoustic expert John Ford have shown that not only do resident killer whales have an impressive catalog of underwater calls but they also exhibit subtly different "pronunciation" and "vocabularies" from one orca pod to the next, in much the same way that human accents and use of words vary subtly from one region to another.

Using the metaphor of human language, biologists refer to such group-specific variations on a species' basic repertoire of calls as "dialects." Thus, a resident killer whale dialect is a particular set of between seven and seventeen discrete calls associated with a given pod. And according to Ford, "early results from research in Norway, Iceland, Alaska and the sub-antarctic indicate that local vocalizations with pod-specific dialects may be typical of killer whales wherever they are found."

Within the family groups of a pod, calves presumably learn calls by mimicking their mothers (possibly even in utero), as well as by listening to other group members. So even though all members of a given pod share a common dialect, subtle variations in calls sometimes arise in subpods as a result of times spent travelling away from the pod. Nonetheless, a pod's distinctive dialect is a crucial unifying force in orca society. It is,

PAGES 78–79:

Orcas on the move.

THOMAS KITCHIN/FIRST LIGHT

in effect, an acoustic extended-family badge, instantly confirming to all within hearing distance the biological, as well as social, affiliation of all who "speak" it. Recent studies suggest that transient killer whales also communicate vocally with other members of their groups. But perhaps because these groups lack the stable, fixed membership of their resident cousins, researchers are not finding the same neat array of dialects that they have found in resident killer whale society.

The social bonds that bind transient orcas seem to be continuously in flux. As a result, the entire population appears to share the same fairly uniform set of calls. Transient killer whales also rely on a smaller repertoire of calls—generally a half-dozen or less—than their more talkative resident kin. And because of the stealth with which transients stalk seals and other wary warm-blooded prey, they use this reduced vocabulary of calls far less frequently than do their fish-eating resident cousins. In fact, the recent evolutionary paths of these two subspecies have diverged so much that they no longer share a single call.

Orca Conversations

IF KILLER WHALES "CONVERSE" WITH ONE ANOTHER IN THE DISTINCTIVE dialects of their pods, what could they possibly be saying?

There is no compelling evidence that wild orcas routinely exchange complex, symbol-laden linguistic messages steeped in abstract details about themselves and their watery world. On the contrary, given the highly stereotyped and often repetitive nature of most recorded orca exchanges, it is likely that killer whale vocalizations serve a far more limited function than does human language.

But this in no way diminishes the vital role such acoustic exchanges must play in the intricate social lives of orcas. Orca squeals and squawks may serve, as suggested earlier, as an instant vocal update on the current status of the whale emitting the call. For embedded in the sonic signature of each call—in its quantitative features, such as pitch, loudness and harmonic structure, as well as in its more qualitative features, such as timbre, urgency and robustness—may lie a wealth of instantly understandable information about the caller. Calls are likely, for instance, to contain clues to the identity of the individual caller, to the caller's emotional state and even to what the caller is doing. These calls may also reveal the caller's age, sex and physical condition, in much the same way that one can often instantly determine that the voice of the operator on the telephone probably belongs to a middle-aged woman who, sounding a bit weary after a long day at work, is recovering from a bad cold.

If killer whale calls contain a wealth of information about individual identity and emotional state, they are not necessarily entirely devoid of conceptual meaning. Recent studies have shown that the vocalizations of African vervet monkeys, among other species, for example, can convey precise information about the *kind* of predator that is in the vicinity (through, for example, a characteristic "eagle-alarm" call). And decades of research on captive bottlenose dolphins continue to suggest that these animals, like chimpanzees and gorillas, are often capable of remarkable feats using artificial human linguistic systems to interact with researchers. Louis Herman, at the University of Hawaii, for example, has carried out experiments showing that captive bottlenose dolphins are remarkably adept at learning to respond to simple computer-generated sentences using sounds to represent some forty to fifty verbs and nouns.

To date, the acoustic communication skills of killer whales have not been subjected to similar scrutiny. But they could well prove comparable. If so, it is at least conceivable that orca vocal exchanges occasionally harbour far more than rudimentary clues to individual identity, mood or action. They could also bear semantic references to, for example, specific prey species, familiar hunting strategies or even fellow pod members, thereby vastly expanding a killer whale pod's collective mental map of its world and enhancing the survival of its members.

OVERLEAF:

The fat-cushioned, immobile face of a killer whale may seem to us all but devoid of expression. But an orca's eyes, some say, often reveal valuable clues to the dolphin's internal emotional state. FRANS LANTING / MINDEN PICTURES

CHAPTER FIVE

IMAGINING ORCA

WHALES HAVE HAD THEIR MOST ADVANCED BRAINS

FOR ALMOST THIRTY MILLION YEARS. OUR SPECIES HAS

EXISTED FOR ABOUT ONE-THOUSANDTH OF THAT TIME.

WE HAVE A LOT TO LEARN FROM WHALES.

—Roger Payne, *Among Whales*, 1995

TO SAY THAT DOLPHINS ECHOLOCATE IS LIKE SAYING

MICHELANGELO PAINTED CHURCH CEILINGS.

—Patrick W. B. Moore, *Dolphin Societies: Discoveries and Puzzles*, 1991

THE KILLER WHALE'S BRAIN

THE BIG, HIGHLY CONVOLUTED BRAIN OF MOST DOLPHINS IS AN IMPRESSIVE organ in size, shape and structural complexity. And of all dolphin brains, the brain of the killer whale, along with that of the bottlenose dolphin and a few others, has drawn particular attention from scientists and nonscientists alike.

In *Hamlet*, Shakespeare refers to human beings as the "paragon of animals." Scientists have historically granted the human brain an exalted status in the kingdom of animals based on its disproportionate size, compared with body weight; its greatly expanded outer rind, or cortex; and its deeply fissured, or convoluted, surface.

But the brains of dolphins, including killer whales, share many of these vaunted "human" attributes. Furthermore, the dolphin "experiment" in the evolution of big mammalian brains made its appearance tens of millions of years before the hominid one did. So we should not be surprised by the number of quite distinctive anatomical features in orca's highly advanced brain.

First, there are its sheer dimensions. The dolphin brain is wider than it is long, in contrast to typical mammalian brains. And it is enormous. The brain of an adult orca can weigh up to 6 kilograms (over 13 pounds). This is about four times heavier than the brain of an average bottlenose dolphin and more than three times heavier than a human brain. But brain size alone, we now know, is not a reliable indicator of intelligence.

"Intelligence," of course, remains an elusive concept—one that, at the very least, must be redefined to fit each species' sensory reality. Nonetheless, classical animal "IQ" tests have generally ranked dolphin mental capacities somewhere between those of dogs and chimpanzees. Still, there are tantalizing signs of dolphin mental prowess in somewhat improved indices of animal "braininess," such as the simple ratio of brain weight to spinal cord weight. For example, the bottlenose dolphin, a close cousin of the killer whale, has been calculated to have a ratio of about 40:1; a horse, about 2.5:1; a cat, about 5:1; an ape, about 8:1; and humans, about 50:1. Thus, by this measure at least, the brains of dolphins, adjusting for obvious differences in body weight, seem to surpass those of every mammalian rival except for *Homo sapiens*.

Second, the paired cerebral hemispheres of orca's brain, the seat of many of the most advanced mental processes in humans, are exceptionally large and well developed. In fact, in some dolphin species, the cerebral cortex, the outer and evolutionarily most recent layer of the brain, may actually be more convoluted than that of any other ani-

Killer whales rest, sometimes for hours at a time, by floating or swimming lazily near the surface in compact family groups maintained by sight, touch and sporadic calls. Based on brain recordings showing REM (rapid-eye-movement) wave patterns in vigilant orcas as they fitfully doze, they may even dream. FRANS LANTING/MINDEN PICTURES

mal species on Earth—including *Homo sapiens*. And the total surface area of the bottlenose dolphin's sprawling brain cortex has been reported to be half again as expansive as that of the venerable human cortex (although only perhaps half as thick).

Third, in dolphins, the microscopic structure of the cortex, so crucial to high-level integration of nerve signals, also differs in important ways from that of the human cortex. Reflecting its recent independent evolutionary past, it appears more diffuse, lacking the neat, layer-cake-like laminations of our own cortical grey matter—a feature that allies it more with the brains of modern bats and hedgehogs than with those of modern primates.

Fourth, the dolphin brain is specially adapted to process sound. Auditory nerve fibres, for example, tend to be larger in diameter, enabling them to transmit signals more rapidly in the dolphin central nervous system than in our own. Presumably the dolphin brain also possesses special sensory nerve cells, similar to those found in echolocating bats, tuned to detect and analyze subtle differences in a broad spectrum of sounds extending far beyond the limits of human hearing. And the dolphin brain seems to have the capacity to transform incoming sounds into a seamless acoustic image of the animal's surroundings.

Although more decades of study are required to understand the mental capacities of the killer whale, we can at least try to *imagine* possible dimensions of dolphin perception and sensory reality. And we can try to reimagine them anew each time we learn a little bit more.

But our task will remain forever unfinished. For as biologist and author Loren Eiseley laments in a memorable essay titled "The Long Loneliness," "It is difficult for us to visualize another kind of lonely, almost disembodied intelligence floating in the wavering green fairyland of the sea—an intelligence possibly comparable to our own."

KILLER WHALE SENSES
IF THE SENSORY EXPERIENCE OF KILLER WHALES OCCURS PRIMARILY IN SOUND— through ordinary hearing, as well as echolocation—what role might the other senses play in their lives?

Consider vision. The sense of sight is well developed in killer whales. But sunlight rapidly dissipates in the sea, and in deeper waters almost total darkness reigns. Given the effects of low light, wave action and natural turbidity from algae and debris, even in surface waters visibility may often be reduced to 50 metres (160 feet) or less. At night (a time when orcas are still active) it can approach zero. Consequently, in the sensory world of the killer whale, sight must generally supplement, rather than substitute for, sound.

Nonetheless, killer whales possess keen vision—both in water and in air—with a capacity to discriminate fine detail that is perhaps comparable to that of a domestic cat. In addition, orca eyes must withstand a number of extremely demanding underwater conditions, from deep dives into dim waters and high-speed chases to occasional bouts of aerial scanning, when a whale spy hops, lifting its head out of the water to visually survey its surroundings.

It is uncertain whether killer whales perceive their world in bright colours or in stark monochromes. Nonetheless, their eyes are probably well equipped to detect rapid movements and fleeting events occurring in the animal's immediate surroundings. And, given their position on the head, they probably provide excellent binocular vision, at least in a downward direction.

Like most cetaceans, orcas are also known to be exquisitely sensitive to touch. Their skin is richly endowed with nerve endings, particularly around the eyes, face, snout and blowhole, as well as in the area of the male and female genital openings. The importance of touch is revealed almost daily in killer whale lives. As it surfaces to breathe, an orca is probably able to precisely time its blows and dives in part by using tactile signals from skin on its face, dorsal fin and blowhole. And a swimming whale almost certainly adjusts its movements in part according to subtle shifts in water pressure, monitored by nerve endings on its flippers, tail flukes and other body parts. It may even rely on such messages (along with visual and acoustic cues) to help synchronize its dives and blows, as well as to maintain orderly travelling formations with other members of its group.

It is also the sense of touch that instantly alerts a mother orca to her hungry calf's attempts to suckle. Touch guides the dialogue of nudges, nibbles and fore-flipper caresses that nurture the long, intimate bond between mother and young. One orca may rake its teeth across the back of another orca, and juvenile males may sensuously roll, wrestle

A killer whale calf normally suckles for at least a year. Brief underwater bouts of nursing occur when a young calf abandons its energy-conserving slipstream position near its mother's dorsal fin to suck jets of rich, fat-laden milk from one of her two retractable abdominal nipples.
JOHN FORD / URSUS PHOTOGRAPHY

Water-borne sound reflects off objects in very different ways from light. Because skin, muscle and fat tissues are almost transparent to echolocation clicks, killer whale biosonar probably creates images of other animals that highlight dense bony structures and air-filled cavities.

As a result, an actively echolocating orca in dim waters may actually perceive a family member not as a big, black-and-white dolphin (as it might visu-ally) but rather as an X-ray-like image, complete with teeth, skeleton, digestive tract and lungs. It is even conceivable that killer whales use such intimate sonic snapshots to monitor one another's visceral changes, thereby providing useful clues to the identity, emotional state or even physical condition of another whale.

Killer whales may also use quite different strategies of echolocation, supplemented by ordinary sight and hearing, depending on their particular

and cavort with each other, often displaying erections. And of course there is the clandestine, tactile underwater ballet of killer whale copulation itself.

The possible roles of smell and taste are more elusive. Brain studies suggest that the ancestors of modern dolphins probably lost the olfactory sense so vital to many land mammals during their gradual adaptation to life beneath the sea. Dolphins apparently do possess some form of taste, relying on sensors on the tongue to detect certain chemicals dissolved in sea water. It is possible that orcas monitor underwater clouds of freshly excreted urine or feces, which are potentially laden with valuable chemical clues to a fellow animal's physical condition, sex, reproductive status and even identity. Taste could be used to detect submarine trails of chemical debris left by distant schools of fish or other marine prey (long before such animals could be spotted by echolocation), in much the same way that a wolf tracks the spoor of an unseen herd of caribou. Or killer whales might even use taste to pick up useful underwater navigational cues—complementing more powerful acoustic and visual clues. Among them: the brackish "whiff" of a familiar inlet or the delicate "fragrance" of a distant underwater meadow of undulating eelgrass.

ECHOLOCATION: PICTURES OF SOUND

TO SURVIVE IN TURBID SEAS, THE INKY WATERS OF NIGHT AND OCEAN DEPTHS, killer whales and their kin rely on an extraordinarily well developed form of hearing. Like bats, shrews and a few other mammals and birds, killer whales and other toothed whales have, over time, developed extremely sensitive sensory systems based on sound.

The basic principle of biological sonar, or echolocation, is similar to that of the sonar systems in submarines and other ships, which scan their undersea surroundings using patterns of echoes generated by short pulses of sound. Scientists have estimated that the capabilities of the dolphin's echolocation apparatus could exceed up to tenfold those of most electronically engineered sonar equipment on ships.

Like vision, echolocation detects energy that has been reflected or scattered by objects in its path. Whereas vision relies on "echoes" of light, echolocation relies on echoes of sound. Another difference is that animal sight depends largely on a single, natural, external source of illuminating energy—the sun. Animal echolocation, in contrast, depends on a creature's own internal source of high-pitched vocalizations, which acoustically "light up" its world (although animals with biosonar are also superbly equipped to passively listen to their surroundings without generating clicks.)

The whale first emits a stream of staccato, high-frequency sounds, each lasting mere milliseconds. These sounds are produced in specialized structures in the nasal passages lying beneath the whale's blowhole or possibly deeper, in the larynx, or windpipe, itself. It is possible that concave surfaces of the skull and upper jaw create a natural parabolic reflector, directing the exiting stream of clicks forward, like a broad searchlight beam aimed in the direction of the animal's path.

Before leaving the dolphin's head region, the clicks pass through the fat-laden mound in the forehead known as the melon. This fatty tissue apparently slows down the sounds slightly, thereby refracting their paths in much the same way that a convex lens of glass refracts light passing through it. Thus, the melon may serve as an acoustic "lens," concentrating the diffuse sound "rays" into a tightly focussed cone of clicks that sweeps ahead of the whale like an invisible searchlight.

When the beam of this sonic searchlight strikes an object—such as a nearby fish, kelp frond or family member—a portion of its energy is reflected back towards the dolphin as a faint echo. Most rebounding sonar clicks do not pass directly through the ear canals; in fact, in cetaceans the external ear opening has been drastically reduced to a mere pinhole behind each eye, and the ear passages, plugged with wax, are barely functional.

Instead, returning echoes are channelled to the brain through the thin, drumlike bony walls of the left and right outer surfaces of the dolphin's lower jaw. From here sounds are transmitted along the length of the jaw bones, through natural acoustic conduits formed by their fluid, fat-filled cores. Eventually they reach the delicate paired sensory organs of the middle ear lying on either side of the skull, not far from the base of the brain.

Here the signals, encoded with detailed information about objects off which they rebound, are instantly converted into high-speed sensory nerve impulses. These, in turn, are conducted along neural circuits to the cortex and other auditory processing areas of an orca's complex brain. In ways that are still largely mysterious, the acoustic

predatory lifestyle. According to a recent study by Canadian killer whale researcher Lance Barrett-Lennard, fish-eating resident killer whales, which emit sonar clicks fairly frequently as they hunt for prey, may identify and track preferred species of salmon based in part on the unique acoustic characteristics of a fish's buoyant swim bladder.

In contrast, seal-eating transient killer whales emit clicks far more sparingly, presumably to avoid early detection by wary prey, since these whales repeatedly patrol familiar concentrations of sea mammals along traditional routes that Barrett-Lennard aptly compares to trap lines.

To spot a vulnerable young harbour seal pup, for instance, as it playfully splashes at the water's edge, a transient orca probably relies largely on its keen sense of hearing, as well as sight. The whale might also issue isolated sonar clicks to quickly confirm that based on acoustic reflections from its lungs, a swimming target is, in fact, a tasty marine mammal.

centres of orca's brain then analyze and integrate these data, transforming sound to picture, much as clinical ultrasound instruments produce an image of a living human fetus inside its mother's womb.

Sound travels at a fairly constant speed in water (roughly four times faster than in air). Consequently, echoes from a dolphin's train of high-frequency clicks ricocheting off an object carry considerable information about its distance, speed, size, shape, texture and even composition. By varying the pitch, loudness or duration of its click, as well as the angle and breadth of the sonar spotlight beam itself, a dolphin can also "zoom in" on parts of the object, scrutinizing it with sound much as we might visually scrutinize it with a beam of light.

A killer whale's ability to transform staccato echoes into acoustic "pictures" may seem like an incredible mental feat. And of course it is. But our own ability (and an orca's too, whenever it uses vision), to integrate patterns of reflected light into seamless, three-dimensional images of our surroundings is no less miraculous. Moreover, in his book *Animal Minds*, eminent American animal behaviourist Donald Griffin suggests that animal consciousness, in all its rich diversity, may well be capable of conjuring up vivid, three-dimensional mental images of the world based not just on sound or light but also on heat, odours and other sensory input.

It is possible that the killer whale not only can sonically "see" its surroundings in detailed "sound pictures" but also can choose to see them simultaneously as pictures of light. We humans, for all our real and illusory mental prowess, are, of course, utterly incapable of duplicating such a stupendous, if still speculative, sensory feat.

Evolution has superbly equipped killer whales to perceive their surroundings both acoustically, as ghostly sonic images of kelp fronds and passing fish schools, and visually, illuminated by shimmering shafts of sunlight in algae-fogged seas. JIM BORROWMAN/ NOOMAS PHOTOGRAPHY

FACING PAGE:

In a spectacular display, a pair of orcas spy hops in tamdem. KELLEY BALCOMB-BARTOK

A killer whale toys with golden strands of kelp, draping it over sensitive areas of skin surrounding its dorsal fin. The often energetic play activities of young orcas may appear superficially devoid of survival value. But, as in humans, they are probably vital to mental, physical and social development. JEFF FOOTT/ JEFF FOOTT PRODUCTIONS

PAGE 94:

A killer whale echolocates by emitting streams of high-pitched clicks from its bulging forehead, or melon. It then detects echoes reflecting off any object in their path and mentally transforms them into instant "soundpictures." JEFF FOOTT/JEFF FOOTT PRODUCTIONS

GO TO THE PINE IF YOU WANT TO LEARN ABOUT THE

PINE, OR THE BAMBOO, IF YOU WANT TO LEARN ABOUT

THE BAMBOO. AND IN DOING SO, YOU MUST LEAVE

YOUR SUBJECTIVE PREOCCUPATION WITH YOURSELF.

OTHERWISE YOU IMPOSE YOURSELF ON THE OBJECT

AND DO NOT LEARN. YOUR POETRY ISSUES OF ITS OWN

ACCORD WHEN YOU AND THE OBJECT HAVE BECOME ONE.

—Matsuo Basho, seventeenth-century Japanese Buddhist monk and wandering poet

TODAY THE HISTORIC DEMONIZATION OF THE KILLER WHALE HAS ALL BUT SUB-sided. Yet we must still address challenging issues about our future relationship with this species.

Although orca populations around the world appear to be neither endangered nor systematically exploited, they do face certain long-term perils. Like other cetaceans, orcas swim through seas that may be spiked with toxic industrial wastes, including PCBs and heavy metals. Data on toxic damage to killer whale populations are scarce. But as top predators in the marine food chain, orcas are especially prone to accumulating such poisons in their blubber, where they could eventually find expression in cancers, repro-ductive failures or weakened immune systems.

As the *Exxon Valdez* oil spill in Alaska's Prince William Sound in March 1989 demonstrated, killer whales are also affected by oil pollution. Although the precise effect of this environmental catastrophe on local resident and transient orcas may never be fully known, recent studies suggest that killer whales probably do not detour oiled waters and are therefore likely to be exposed to toxic pollutants directly, as well as by eating oil-contaminated prey. Circumstantial evidence suggests that at least fourteen killer whales in the area may have died directly or indirectly as a result of the spill.

Because killer whales rely on underwater sounds both to echolocate and to com-municate with one another, they could be negatively affected by rising levels of noise pollution. Exposed to the growing din of marine vessel traffic and industrial activities, orca predatory and social behaviour could be acoustically disturbed in ways that are not yet fully understood. The growing hordes of whale watchers and kayakers, including some of the killer whale's most fervent admirers, may also inadvertently be responsible for short-term disturbances of orcas, particularly in highly accessible whale populations in the Pacific Northwest.

Killer whales have also endured a long, uneasy relationship with the world's com-mercial fishing industries, which have often looked on this marine carnivore as "unfair" economic competition rather than as a creature fully entitled to live and flourish. When the food preferences of killer whales are known to include commercially valuable fish stocks such as chinook salmon runs off the coast of British Columbia, Washington and Alaska or schools of herring off the Norwegian coast, who will speak for orcas if imper-illed commercial fisheries one day falter or even totally collapse?

Killer whales around the world may also face long-term threats from forces such

FACING PAGE:

Many of us feel an inexpressible sense of kinship—however separate our worlds—in the presence of both cap-tive and wild killer whales. But a killer whale compelled to live out its life in a shallow, acoustically impoverished aquarium pool—so unlike the deep open waters where it belongs—may, in some sense, no longer be "a complete whale." JEFF FOOTT/JEFF FOOTT PRODUCTIONS

as global warming, ozone depletion and habitat loss arising from human overpopulation and unchecked industrial growth. How might unexpected changes in ocean currents, food resources or access to traditional travel routes and feeding grounds affect the survival of orca populations in the decades to come?

We must also face pressing ethical questions about our right to capture and display such an intelligent, mobile and social mammal in our zoos and aquariums, whether for education, entertainment or our own sense of superiority over other life forms. Today we stand at a historical crossroads in our relationship with the killer whale. Despite areas of ignorance, we simply know too much about the extraordinary biological capacities and basic needs of wild killer whales to continue to try to justify their routine lifelong imprisonment in cramped, acoustically and socially austere aquatic "cells."

It is not a matter of assessing blame. It is probably true that the public has learned a great deal by viewing captive killer whales in aquariums over the past quarter century and that public consciousness about dolphins, porpoises and whales has increased exponentially during that period. But it is time for us to search for ways to build a new and more respectful relationship with *Orcinus orca*.

The recent history of this shift in public perceptions about killer whales and their kin has been ably recounted in a review written by Victor Scheffer, an international authority on marine mammals now in his eighties and, in recent years, an important critic of killer whale captivity, and Stephen Kellert, a professor of forestry and environmental studies at Yale. Aptly titled "The Changing Place of Marine Mammals in American Thought," it argues that the killer whale and other cetaceans have been the beneficiaries of a monumental transition in public consciousness about conservation. In the process, the public has seized on the luminous image of cetaceans as emblematic of the very essence of freedom and wildness in nature. "The Great Whale—a generic concept," they state, "continues to be an umbrella symbol of a widespread urge to protect populations, to treat animals with respect, and even to concede them certain rights which humans take for granted."

Having lived through this transition myself, I too, along with growing numbers of others, have gradually come to see limits on the value of casually keeping cetaceans in captivity. I believe that we can no longer rest on the historically convenient illusion that by peering through glass walls at killer whales awkwardly confined in the aquatic cages of some of our most cherished institutions of environmental education, the public is somehow getting to "know" the killer whale. For an orca, forced to live out its life, in the words of Victor Scheffer, in "barren, resounding shallow pools grossly unlike the deep and open waters where they belong," is, in some sense, no longer "a complete whale." At the same time, it would be a serious mistake to let the contentious issue of the captivity of a few whales eclipse the larger issue of protecting the world's population of wild whales.

Nowhere have I encountered a more jewel-like crystallization of the inherent injustice, however well intentioned, of continuing to cage a creature as sophisticated as the killer whale than in the German poet Rainer Maria Rilke's poem about another captive carnivore, entitled "The Panther." Penned in the first decade of this century, following his own dispiriting visit to a Paris zoo, it contains the following luminous passage:

> *As he paces in cramped circles, over and over,*
> *the movement of his powerful soft strides*
> *is like a ritual dance around a centre*
> *in which a mighty will stands paralyzed.*

For me, this poem is also a fitting epitaph for all captive killer whales denied access to their natural surroundings. For when we watch a captive orca with a deformed dorsal fin swimming endlessly "in cramped circles" in a tiny aquarium pool, isn't what we are really seeing an aquatic version of a "ritual dance around a centre in which a mighty will stands paralyzed"?

To even begin to "know" the killer whale we must somehow avoid reducing this animal to a mere object or abstraction, and we must be willing to accept a measure of mystery. We must approach the animal on its own terms and in natural settings and there permit it to fully engage our hearts, minds and imagination. In the process, we must abandon our blinding human self-absorption and, steeped in orca lore and, if possible, in the wild whale's electrifying presence, permit ourselves to re-imagine all of nature anew.

At the same time, our visions of the killer whale are destined to remain forever fragmentary and in flux. For as breath fogs a mirror, human images of other life forms are inescapably clouded and incomplete. American artist, author and whale expert Richard Ellis neatly sums up our mortal dilemma:

> *The killer whale is not an unreconstructed murderer; neither is it a jolly circus clown, to be made to jump through hoops for our entertainment. The real orca lies somewhere between these two extremes; or maybe we will find that it is beyond the scope of our understanding.*

No human being can ever fully fathom
the interior thoughts, feelings and moti-
vations of another species—especially
one as intelligent, socially complex and
elusive as *Orcinus orca.* JEFF FOOTT/JEFF
FOOTT PRODUCTIONS

SELECTED REFERENCES

Baird, R. W., and P. J. Stacey. 1988. "Foraging and Feeding Behavior of Transient Killer Whales." *Whalewatcher* (Journal of American Cetacean Society) 22:11–15.

Balcomb, K. C. 1991. "Kith and Kin of the Killer Whale." *Pacific Discovery* 44(2):8–17.

Balcomb, K. C., J. R. Boran, and S. I. Heimlich. 1982. "Killer Whales in Greater Puget Sound." *Report International Whaling Commission* 32:681–85.

Barrett-Lennard, L. 1992. "Echolocation in Wild Killer Whales *(Orcinus orca)*." Master's thesis. University of British Columbia.

Bigg, M. A., G. M. Ellis, J. K. B. Ford, and K. C. Balcomb. 1987. *Killer Whales: A Study of Their Identification, Genealogy and Natural History in British Columbia and Washington State.* Nanaimo, B.C.: Phantom Press.

Bigg, Michael, P. F. Olesiuk, G. M. Ellis, J. K. B. Ford, and K. C. Balcomb. 1990. "Social Organization and Genealogy of Resident Killer Whales (*Orcinus orca*) in the Coastal Waters of British Columbia and Washington State." *Report International Whaling Commission* 12:383–405.

Boas, Franz. 1930. *The Religion of the Kwakiutl Indians.* Vol. X of Columbia University Contributions to Anthropology, Part 2. New York: Columbia University Press.

Cousteau, J. 1972. *The Whale: Mighty Monarch of the Sea.* Garden City, N.Y.: Doubleday.

Divine, Eleanore, and Martha Clark. 1967. *The Dolphin Smile: Twenty-nine Centuries of Dolphin Lore.* New York: Macmillan; London: Collier-Macmillan.

Dolphin, William F. 1987. "Observations of Humpback Whale, *Megaptera novaengliae*—Killer Whale, *Orcinus orca*, Interactions in Alaska: Comparison with Terrestrial Predator-Prey Relationships." *The Canadian Field-Naturalist* 101(1):70–75.

Eiseley, Loren. 1960-61. "The Long Loneliness." *American Scholar* (Winter): 57-64.

Ellis, Richard. 1982. *Dolphins and Porpoises.* New York: Knopf.

Evans, Peter G. H. 1987. *The Natural History of Whales and Dolphins*. New York: Facts On File.

Ford, John K. B. 1984. "Call Traditions and Dialects of Killer Whales (*Orcinus orca*) in British Columbia." Ph.D. diss., Department of Zoology, University of British Columbia.

————. 1989. "Acoustic Behavior of Resident Killer Whales (*Orcinus orca*) in British Columbia." *Canadian Journal of Zoology* 67:727–45.

————. 1991. "Vocal Traditions among Resident Killer Whales (*Orcinus orca*) in the Coastal Waters of British Columbia." *Canadian Journal of Zoology* 69:1454–83.

————. 1991. "Family Fugues." *Natural History* 3:68–76.

Ford, John K. B., and Deborah Ford. 1981. "The Killer Whales of B.C." *Waters (Journal of the Vancouver Aquarium)* 5(1) (Summer):1–32.

Ford, John K. B., Graeme M. Ellis, and Kenneth C. Balcomb. 1994. *Killer Whales: The Natural History and Genealogy of* Orcinus orca *in British Columbia and Washington State*. Vancouver: University of British Columbia Press; Seattle: University of Washington Press.

Gormley, Gerard. 1990. *Orcas of the Gulf: A Natural History*. Vancouver: Douglas & McIntyre.

Griffin, Donald R. 1992. *Animal Minds*. Chicago: University of Chicago Press.

Heimlich-Boran, James R. 1988. "Behavioral Ecology of Killer Whales (*Orcinus orca*) in the Pacific Northwest." Canadian Journal of Zoology 66:565–78.

Heimlich-Boran, Sara, and James Heimlich-Boran. 1994. *Killer Whales*. Stillwater, Minn.: Voyageur Press.

Hoelzel, A. R. 1991. "Killer Whale Predation on Marine Mammals at Punta Norte, Argentina; Food Sharing, Provisioning and Foraging Strategy." *Behavioral Ecology and Sociobiology* 29(3):197–204.

Hoyt, Erich. 1992. *The Peforming Orca: Why the Show Must Stop*. Bath, Avon, Eng.: Whale and Dolphin Conservation Society.

———. 1990. *The Whale Called Killer*. Camden East, Ont.: Camden House.

Jefferson, T. A., P. J. Stacey, and R.W. Baird. 1991. "A Review of Killer Whale Interactions with Other Marine Mammals: Predation to Co-existence." *Marine Review* 22:151–80.

Kirkevold, Barbara C., and Joan S. Lockard, eds. 1986. *Behavioral Biology of Killer Whales*. New York: Alan R. Liss.

Knudtson, Peter, and David Suzuki. 1992. *Wisdom of the Elders*. Don Mills, Ont.: Stoddart.

Leatherwood, Stephen, and Randall R. Reeves, eds. 1990. *The Bottlenose Dolphin*. San Diego: Academic Press.

Lopez, Barry. 1978. *Of Wolves and Men*. New York: Scribners.

McIntryre, Joan, ed. 1974. *Mind in the Waters: A Book to Celebrate the Consciousness of Whales and Dolphins*. New York: Scribners.

Masson, Jeffrey M., and Susan McCarthy. 1995. *When Elephants Weep: The Emotional Lives of Animals*. New York: Delacorte Press.

Matkin, Craig. 1994. *An Observer's Guide to the Killer Whales of Prince William Sound*. Valdez, Ala.: Prince William Sound Books.

Matkin, Craig, and S. Leatherwood. 1986. "General Biology of Killer Whales." In *Behavioral Biology of Killer Whales,* edited by Stephen Leatherwood and Randall R. Reeves. New York: Alan R. Liss.

Morton, Alexandra. 1991. *Siwiti: A Whale's Story*. Victoria: Orca.

———. 1993. *In the Company of Whales*. Victoria: Orca.

Norris, Kenneth, ed. 1966. *Whales, Dolphins, and Porpoises*. Berkeley and Los Angeles: University of California Press.

Obee, Bruce, and Graeme Ellis. 1992. *Guardians of the Whales: The Quest to Study Whales in the Wild*. Vancouver: Whitecap Books.

Olesiuk, P. F., M. A. Bigg, and G. M. Ellis. 1990. "Life History and Population Dynamics of Resident Killer Whales (*Orcinus orca*) in the Coastal Waters of British Columbia and Washington State." *Report International Whaling Commission* 12:209–43.

Payne, Roger. 1995. *Among Whales*. New York: Scribners.

Pryor, Karen, and Kenneth Norris, eds. 1991. *Dolphin Societies: Discoveries and Puzzles*. Berkeley: University of California Press.

Rilke, Rainer Maria. 1989. *The Selected Poetry of Rainer Maria Rilke*. Edited and translated by Stephen Mitchell. New York: Vintage International.

Scheffer, Victor. 1969. *The Year of the Whale*. New York: Scribners.

————. 1991. "Cetaceans in Captivity." *Whalewatcher* (Fall):20.

Scheffer, Victor B., and Stephen R. Kellert. 1994. "The Changing Place of Marine Mammals in American Thought." Draft, unpublished manuscript (quoted with permission of Victor Scheffer), 87 pp.

Schusterman, Ronald J., Jeannette A. Thomas, and Forrest G. Wood, eds. 1986. *Dolphin Cognition and Behavior: A Comparative Approach*. London: Lawrence Erlbaum.

Slijper, Everhard J. 1976. *Whales and Dolphins*. Ann Arbor: University of Michigan Press.

Tarpy, Cliff. 1993. "Killer Whale Attack." *National Geographic* (April 1, 1993) 155:542–545.

Thomas, Jeanette A., and Ronald A. Kastelein, eds. 1990. *Sensory Abilities of Cetaceans: Laboratory and Field Evidence*. New York and London: Plenum Press.

Walens, Stanley. 1981. *Feasting with Cannibals: An Essay on Kwakiutl Cosmology*. Princeton: Princeton University Press.

Würsig, Bernd. 1979. "Dolphins." *Scientific American*. March: 136–48.

INDEX

Archaeocete, 24
Aristotle, 11

Balcomb, Kenneth, 54
Baleen whales, 7, 10, 14, 24
Barrett-Lennard, Lance, 89
Basho, Matsuo, 95
Behaviour
    aggressive, 2, 11, 18, 57,
       75–76
    birth, 58–59
    breathing, 14, 38–39, 51
    sexual, 51, 57, 87
    social, 48, 75–81, 87
    travelling, 51
Biosonar. See Echolocation
Birth, 11, 22, 38, 54, 58–59, 65,
    66
Blowhole, 23, 24, 34–36, 38, 76,
    87, 89
Blubber, 23, 38, 39, 70, 96
Blue whale, 69–70
Boas, Franz, 14
Brain, 84–86, 89
    acoustic adaptations, 86–89
    anatomy, 84, 89
    cortex, 84–85, 89
    function, 85, 89
    nerve cells, 85
    size, 84
Breaching, 42, 47, 50
Breathing, 14, 38–39, 41, 77, 87
    physiology of, 38
    synchronized, 38–39, 41, 87

Calls, 76–77, 80–81
    discrete, 77
    "residents," 77
    "transients," 80
Calves, 11, 38, 54, 55, 60, 65,
    66, 77, 87
Captivity, 13, 96, 98–100
Cetaceans, 4, 22, 23, 24, 34, 38,
    39, 98
Chemical pollution, 96
Clicks, 34, 76, 77, 88–91, 92
Colour patterns, 43–51, 68
Commercial fishing, 96
Communication, 69, 75–81
Counter-shading, 48
Cousteau, Jacques, 11, 13

Delphinidae, 24
Dialects, 29, 57, 69, 77, 80
Diet, 6, 10, 11, 14, 15, 29, 66,
    68, 71, 96
Distribution, 4–5, 6
Diving, 38, 51
Dorsal fin, 4, 29, 20, 43–44, 58,
    64, 65, 87
Dynasties, 28–29

Echolocation, 24, 86, 88–91, 92,
    96
Eiseley, Loren, 86
Ellis, Graeme, 57
Ellis, Richard, 100
Environmental threats, 96–98,
    100
Evolution of cetaceans, 22–24,
    28
    archaeocetes, 24
    dolphin family, 23–24, 28
    Eocene epoch, 23
    insectivores, 22
    Oligocene epoch, 24
Exxon Valdez oil spill, 42, 96

Family groups. See Matrilineal
    groups
Feeding habits, 6, 14, 66–70,
    71–75, 78

Argentina , 71–75
Baja, Mexico, 69–70
Norway, 66–69
Pacific Northwest, 68–69
Female
    coloration, 51
    life expectancy, 16, 66
    nursing, 65, 87
    reproduction, 65–66
    sexual maturity, 65–66
Ford, John, 57, 77

Groups. See Social organization

Haida, 6, 10, 15–16
Hearing, 73, 86, 88, 89
Heat regulation, 39–43
Herring, 66–69, 96
Hunting. See Feeding habits

Intelligence, 11, 84, 86

Kellert, Stephen, 98
Killer whale
    anatomy 23–24
    behaviour; see Behaviour
    distribution, 4–5, 6
    evolution, 22–28, 30
    life span, 16, 66
    names for, 6–7
    prey, 14, 71
    size, 4, 39
Kwakiutl, 6, 13

Lawrence, D.H., 1
Life stages, 65–66
    adolescence, 65
    adulthood, 65
    infancy, 65
    old age, 15, 16, 66
Lobtailing, 2, 3, 68
Lopez, Barry, 10

FACING PAGE:

An orca breaches in Haro Strait,
between British Columbia and
Washington. THOMAS KITCHIN/
FIRST LIGHT

McCarthy, Cormac, 9
Male
  coloration, 51
  life expectancy, 16, 66
  reproduction, 65
  sexual maturity, 65
Mating. *See* Sexual activity
Matriarchy, 54–57, 63
Matrilineal groups, 26–27, 39, 54–57
Melon, 89, 92
Moore, Patrick, 83
Mysticetes. *See* Baleen whales
Myths about killer whales
  Haida, 10, 15–16
  Kwakiutl, 13–15
  other, 10–13

Noise pollution, 96
Norris, Kenneth, 34

Odontocetes. *See* Toothed whales
"Offshore" killer whales, 29–30
Oil spills, 96
Orca. *See* Killer whale

Payne, Roger, 53, 83
Photoidentification, 28, 54, 65
Play, 63, 65, 75, 92–93
Pliny the Elder, 11
Pods, 26–27, 54–57, 77
Prey species, 14, 71

Races of killer whales, 6, 28–30
  "offshore" killer whales, 29–30
  "resident" killer whales, 6, 28–29, 89
  "transient" killer whales, 6, 29, 43–44, 80, 89
Rilke, Rainer Maria, 99

"Resident" killer whales, 6, 28–29, 89
Resting, 85

Salmon, 2, 6, 10, 14, 15, 29, 30, 66, 68–69, 78, 96
Scammon, Charles, 11
Scheffer, Victor, 21, 98, 99
Sensory capacities, 7, 21, 84, 86–91
  echolocation, 24, 86, 88–91, 92
  hearing, 73, 86, 88
  sight, 7, 86–87, 88, 91
  smell, 88
  taste, 88
  touch, 60, 87
Sexual activity, 51
Sleep. *See* Resting
Social organization, 11, 28–29, 54–57
  dynasties, 28–29
  matrilineal groups, 26–27, 39, 54–57
  pods 26–27, 54–57, 77
  subpods, 54–57, 77
  superpods, 57
Sonar. *see* Echolocation
Sound pictures, 86, 88–91, 92
Speed swimming, 66, 67
Spong, Paul, 33
Spy hopping, 87, 90–91
Subpods, 54–57, 77
Superpods, 57
Swimming, 38–39, 51, 66, 67, 87

Teeth, 24–25, 51, 70, 75, 76, 87
Thermoregulation. *See* Heat regulation
Toothed whales, 24, 88

Tourism, 96
"Transient" killer whales, 43–44, 80, 89
Vision, 7, 86–87, 88, 91
Vocalization, 34, 37, 76–77, 80–81
  dialects, 29, 57, 69, 77, 80
  mechanism, 34, 76
  "residents," 29, 77, 80
  "transients," 29, 80

Wa-'sgo,o', 15–16
Whale. *See* Cetaceans
Whaling, 13